AMBITION
BLACK+WHITE

THE FEMINIST NARRATIVE REVISED

AMBITION IN BLACK+WHITE

THE FEMINIST NARRATIVE REVISED

MELINDA MARSHALL
TAI WINGFIELD

*Featuring profiles of Sylvia Ann Hewlett,
Mellody Hobson, and Charlene Drew Jarvis*

CENTER
FOR TALENT
INNOVATION

This is a Center for Talent Innovation Publication

A Vireo Book | Rare Bird Books
453 South Spring Street, Suite 302
Los Angeles, CA 90013
rarebirdbooks.com

FIRST TRADE PAPERBACK ORIGINAL EDITION

Set in Minion
Printed in the United States

10 9 8 7 6 5 4 3 2 1

Publisher's Cataloging-in-Publication data

Names: Marshall, Melinda, author | Wingfield, Tai, author.
Title: Ambition in black and white : the feminist narrative revised / by Melinda
Marshall and Tai Wingfield.
Description: Includes bibliographical references and index. | First Trade
Paperback Original Edition. | A Vireo Book. | New York [New York] ; Los
Angeles [California] : Rare Bird Books, 2016.
Identifiers: ISBN 978-1-942600-79-4
Subjects: LCSH Feminism. | Feminists. | African American feminists. | African
Americans—Race identity. | Sex role—United States. | Women's studies—
United States. |Racism—United States. | Identity politics—United States. |
African Americans—Economic conditions. | Women—Employment—United
States. | BISAC SOCIAL SCIENCE / Feminism & Feminist Theory | SOCIAL
SCIENCE / Ethnic Studies / African American Studies | SOCIAL SCIENCE /
Women's Studies | BUSINESS & ECONOMICS / Women in Business.
Classification: LCC HD6095 .M29 2016 | DDC 331.4/0973—dc23

To all the women, black and white, who fought fearlessly to ensure we could have a voice.

PROJECT TEAM

Project Lead

Sylvia Ann Hewlett, Founder and CEO

Quantitative Research

Laura Sherbin, CFO and Director of Research

Pooja Jain-Link, Senior Research Associate

Charlene Thrope, Research Associate

Qualitative Research

Anna Weerasinghe, Fellow

Production

Isis Fabian, Research Associate

Catherine Chapman, Research Associate

Communications

Silvia Marte, Communications Associate

CONTENTS

PROLOGUE

Different Pasts, Different Starting Gates

"We can no longer ignore that voice within women that says: 'I want something more than my husband and my children and my home.'" [1]

These words, written by Betty Friedan in 1963, galvanized the movement that reshaped female aspirations, launched women into the workforce, and changed the course of history. [2] The "problem that has no name," as she described women's malaise, branded the ensuing movement as feminism.

Yet from the get-go, Friedan's vision of feminism was not universal. While white, middle-class women framed access to work outside the home as a form of liberation, black women yearned to be liberated from work—from low-paying jobs with poor working conditions where they had little to no opportunity for advancement. As black feminist author and activist bell hooks challenged, "[Friedan] did not tell readers whether it was more fulfilling to be a maid, a babysitter, a factory worker, a clerk, or a prostitute than to be a leisure-class housewife." [3] For the vast majority of black women in 1963, the work available to them was a source of oppression, not liberation; a necessity, not a luxury; a constraint on their fulfillment, not an avenue toward it.

This is not to say that black women had no part in the feminist movement of the 1960s. On the contrary, black women were, in fact, on the frontlines of not one, but *two* fights for equal rights in the mid-twentieth century. Many black feminists stretched their activism to push for the rights for both women and blacks, often from the margins of both movements. Some black feminists were directly involved in the women's liberation movement, like Civil Rights activist and lawyer Pauli Murray, who cofounded the National Organization for Women (NOW) in 1966 alongside Friedan, and *Ms. Magazine* cocreator Dorothy Pitman Hughes, who collaborated closely with Gloria Steinem to found the Women's Action Alliance; others campaigned for the rights of black women specifically, such as bell hooks and womanist author and activist Alice Walker.[4] Many of the most influential black feminists, including Frances Beale, Angela Davis, Claudia Jones, Florynce Kennedy and Cellestine Ware, to name just a few, identified more closely with the fight for Civil Rights than with women's liberation, but their leadership in the Black Power movement wasn't lost on the leaders of the women's movement.[5] As Gloria Steinem reflected in a 2015 interview, "I learned feminism largely from black women. Women of color basically invented feminism."[6]

What united these early black and white feminist leaders was their quest for equality. Pan-Africanist writer and political activist Amy Jacques Garvey presaged Friedan by several decades when she wrote that the modern woman "prefers to be a bread-winner than a half-starved wife at home."[7] Yet white women's career-minded approach to this shared dream grated on black women, as it glossed over glaring racial inequities. As Jacques Garvey pointed out, "White women have greater opportunities to display their ability because of the standing of both races…yet who is more deserving of admiration than the black woman, she who has borne the rigors of slavery, the deprivations consequent on a pauperized race, and the indignities heaped upon a weak and defenseless people?"[8]

What separated black and white feminists was not the destination they envisioned, but rather where they began and the steps they perceived as necessary to attain their goal. "I saw white women as having privilege," observes former Washington, DC Councilwoman Charlene Drew Jarvis. "We were not starting at the same place." Indeed, black women struggled even to be seen as women, let alone as women who deserved more respect and accommodation from men. As Sojourner Truth, one of the founding mothers of feminism, observed in 1851, "That man over there says that women need to be helped into carriages, and lifted over ditches, and to have the best place everywhere. Nobody ever helps me into carriages, or over mud puddles, or gives me any best place! And ain't I a woman? Look at me! Look at my arm! I have ploughed and planted, and gathered into barns, and no man could head me! And ain't I a woman?"[9]

Different starting gates inspired separate strategies for change, ultimately setting black and white women on divergent paths towards empowerment in the workplace and beyond.[10]

WOMEN'S WORK

In her 2014 speech in acceptance of the *Hollywood Reporter*'s Sherry Lansing Leadership award, Shonda Rhimes gave Hollywood women a congratulatory pat on the back. "Thirty years ago, I'd think maybe there'd be a thousand secretaries fending off their handsy bosses back at the office, and about two women in Hollywood in this room," Rhimes said. Then she observed, "And if I were here, I would be serving breakfast."[11]

Rhimes's point—that between then and now, women have made extraordinary progress—serves to underscore not just white and black women's achievements, but also the chasm between their trajectories. Thirty years ago, a handful of white women had managed to battle their way to the top in a few professions, notably entertainment and media, with the majority forced to choose between becoming secretaries and staying home with their children. Most black women didn't even have *that* choice.

The contrast between the experience of white and black working women in the early twentieth century is stark. White women's path into the workplace is a now-familiar story: when World War II emptied factories and offices of men, women were able to enter male-dominated occupations for the first time.[12] From manufacturing planes to piloting them, and from putting out newspapers to practicing medicine, Rosie the Riveter broke down workplace barriers in the name of patriotism. By the 1950s, however, the influx of recently-returned men forced many of these women to exit the workforce.[13] Those who could afford to leave became housewives and stay-at-home mothers, setting the stage for both America's burgeoning middle class and for Friedan's "problem that has no name."[14]

Black women also saw an occupational shift during the war: many left sharecropping—an exploitative system of plantation farming whose roots extended back into slavery—to work in factories or institutions like schools and hospitals.[15] But most of the industries that had welcomed white women as skilled or semi-skilled laborers were not willing to hire black women,[16] as Maya Angelou discovered when, in wartime San Francisco, she went to the railway personnel office to apply for a job as streetcar conductor. "The receptionist was not innocent and neither was I," she writes. "The whole charade we had played out in that crummy waiting room had directly to do with me, Black, and her, white."[17]

Angelou paid innumerable visits to that office before she finally became San Francisco's first black streetcar conductor. Most black women were not so lucky. They had to settle for low-paying, dangerous, or demeaning jobs with no chance of advancement. In airplane assembly plants, for example, black women suffocated in unventilated "dope rooms" full of noxious glue fumes; in sintering plants, they were baked in the heat of blasting furnaces and coated in iron ore dust.[18] In safer venues, like hospitals, black women were confined to undesirable roles such as those in laundry and janitorial services.[19] When the men returned from the front, moreover, working black women didn't go home. As they had before the war, approximately one third of married black women continued to work outside the home—a rate that far outstripped their married white peers.[20]

As the women's liberation movement picked up steam in the sixties and seventies, black and white women continued to follow different career trajectories. Some white women battled their way into male-dominated workspaces, seeking liberation from suburban homemaking as per Friedan's model. This depiction of white women's working experience is, of course, heavily dependent on a certain level of economic privilege. For the 25 percent of families headed by white women living at or below the poverty line, the story was quite different.[21]

Still, even white women of lesser means faced fewer barriers to success than their black peers. Despite avenues provided by the Civil Rights movement and the introduction of Title VII of the Civil Rights Act in

1964, black women faced the double liability of racial discrimination and economic need.[22] Barely four generations had passed since the end of slavery; most black families simply had not had the time to accrue the wealth whites had been building for centuries, and Jim Crow laws continued to limit the ability of black families to accumulate material property.[23] This ongoing racial discrimination and segregation plagued even middle-class black women's entry into the corporate world. Instead, black women like Charlene Drew Jarvis found some success in the public sector, where antidiscrimination policy was more vigorously enforced.[24]

HISTORY MAKER: CHARLENE DREW JARVIS

In 1950, when Charlene Drew Jarvis was eight years old, she lost her father. Dr. Charles Drew, the surgeon and researcher whose work culminated in the American Red Cross Blood Bank, died in a car accident, leaving his wife to raise their four children alone. "I saw how she took charge when he died," Drew Jarvis recalls. "I saw a remarkable woman take on all that she needed to take on to raise four children. She was independent—and very gutsy." Indeed, when Drew Jarvis won acceptance to Oberlin College, she watched in amazement as her mother, a former Spelman College professor, called up classmates of her father's from Amherst to ask if they would help with the tuition. And when her younger sister Sylvia prepared to go to college, her mother called on Eleanor Roosevelt for help. "We didn't know the former first lady!" Drew Jarvis laughs. "That's when I saw in my mother that she was not afraid. She'd find what she needed. And she'd figure out how to get it."

Drew Jarvis's own career honors the examples set by both her mother and father. In 1965, armed with a Master's degree in psychology, she received a pre-doctoral appointment at the National Institute of Health (NIH) in Bethesda, MD. She did not encounter, professionally, efforts to block her progress as an African American. But at Howard University, where she had earned her Master's degree, she did encounter prejudice as a woman. "By that time, I was married and had a child and was pregnant with my second," she says. "The Dean of the School of Social Work thought I couldn't accomplish both being in school and raising children. I thought, 'Yes I can.'" She completed her PhD in neuropsychology at the University of Maryland in 1971 and continued working at the NIH for eight more years. As her father had often told her, "Excellence of performance will overcome any obstacles created by man."

And in the footsteps of her father she might well have continued. But she felt a growing disconnect between her daily reality "in the ivory tower," and the lived experience of those in the black community around her. Ten years after the riots following the 1968 death of Dr. Martin Luther King, Jr., Washington, DC was a predominantly black city surrounding a white Capitol Hill. "I had some responsibility, as an African American," she says. "So I left science and went into public life."

Drew Jarvis was elected to the Council of the District of Columbia to fill a vacated seat in 1979; for the next five terms, from 1980 to 1996, she won reelection to that seat. In 1981, she began her nineteen-year tenure as chair of the Council's Committee on Economic Development. In 1982, she made a valiant attempt to unseat Mayor Marion Barry. With each campaign, she says, she summoned the courage she'd seen her mother demonstrate. "It was gutsy for me to run for public office when I hadn't been in city politics at all," Drew Jarvis reflects. "It was gutsy to leave science and a career for which I had trained to be in the public domain and help address economic vitality problems. And it took a lot of guts to push back, not just on Mayor Barry but also on his administration. I had two little children and a husband at the time. I said to my mother, 'This is a little gutsy! I need you to help me over the next six months.' And she did.

"But I was sure I would prevail," Drew Jarvis continues. "The way I thought of it was, if you set your sights on doing something—and I saw the end goal as really important—then you can succeed. Or as my mother often said, 'Just put one foot in front of the other.'"

Four years before the end of her last term on the Council, Drew Jarvis set her sights on transforming

Southeastern University, an institution founded by the YMCA that was in danger of losing its accreditation. Drew Jarvis saw it as a vital bridge for black businesspeople who knew all about the service they intended to provide, but not the art of doing business—and who lacked access to capital. She saw they might acquire the know-how and the connections they needed if, through Southeastern, they were matched with larger corporations. "So I took over the institution," she says, "and did both jobs as legislator and president for four years." She oversaw Southeastern for nine years before it merged with another institution.

Social goals were paramount in every role she ever held. Even at the NIH, she got involved in minority recruiting, to attract more women and people of color to get into research. "No matter where I was, I was always thinking, how am I advancing people of color?" she observes. "I realized you needed to be at helm, so I looked to be in that position."

Ever eager "to play in the field I was in," Drew Jarvis was determined never to present as a threat, racially. "I wanted outcomes to be equivalent in terms of my own performance," she says. "And because I was conscientious and determined to make a good outcome, maybe I didn't experience the same things as other black women. But I could never be sure I was being evaluated in the same way. And I was afraid the outcome would reflect that." Reflexively she tried to minimize the likelihood of being judged according to stereotype. She recalls a visit to the University of Maryland bookstore where her conversation with the cashier prompted him to say, "Your English is so precise, are you a teacher?" Drew Jarvis realized she had enunciated every word so as not to be perceived, as a minority student, to be lacking in education. "The unconscious things you do, to avoid the stereotype threat," she muses. "I always assumed white people would assume I was not able to compete."

While stereotypes continue to drive unequal outcomes, she says, momentous change is afoot. "We're in revolution in this country with respect to visibility," she observes. "Blacks have a long history of invisibility. Not antagonism, but invisibility. And it seems to me, a curtain has been pulled back. There are many in the white community saying, 'I didn't know; I didn't understand; I didn't see. Now I do.'" As a result of what's become more visible, Drew Jarvis feels that the country may be on a path to greater equity. "People with good intentions have engaged in unconscious biases that have led to outcomes that may look the same as deliberate malevolence—and they're realizing that," she says. "Gradually, it's changing."

Like the public sector, education was an avenue to combat the stigma of race: black women who could afford it began to pursue higher education in greater numbers in the 1970s and '80s, with the integration of schools and the rise of black universities.[25] Yet, even with a college degree in hand, black women still tended to be employed in jobs that offered little in terms of career advancement or income growth.[26] For example, in the field of clerical work—a "pink collar" career that only became accessible to black women in the latter half of the twentieth century—black women were vastly overrepresented in low-skill, low-pay occupations, such as file clerk and keypunch operator.[27] And this despite the likelihood, as our interviewees observe, that these black women held college degrees.[28]

HISTORY MAKER: GERI THOMAS

In the summer of 1970, between her freshman and sophomore years at Georgia State University, Geri Thomas applied for temporary jobs at three businesses: a retail establishment, Southern Bell Telephone and Telegraph Company, and Citizens and Southern National Bank. Thomas got offers from all three companies. She accepted the bank's offer, which was to work in operations, managing people's accounts. "I'm going to have to straighten my hair," Thomas, who wore a large Afro, remembers telling her mother.

She kept her Afro. She also stayed on that fall. Thomas would, in fact, stay on at the bank for the next forty-five years, working her way from operations at Citizens and Southern to global chief diversity officer at what became, through a series of mergers, Bank of America. When Thomas retired from the bank in 2016, it was as a business leader—the first woman in her family, and among the first black women of her generation, to be in business, let alone to be an executive in a multinational corporation.

None of that was apparent to her that summer of 1970, however. Racism was rampant, despite the legal protections afforded by the Civil Rights Act of 1964. While black people worked at the bank, they didn't hold supervisory roles, despite the fact that many had college degrees. "Men and women who were white didn't have degrees, the chief credit officer didn't have a degree," she says, "so that was an aha moment: clearly the standards were different."

Racism had constrained her parents' career paths, even though her mother was college-educated. Middle-class black women could be leaders in education or health, as head nurses or school principals, provided they worked in all-black hospitals or schools. Because her mother, a teacher, worked outside the home, Thomas never doubted she would, as well; and because racial barriers were lifting, she saw no reason to limit her aspirations. "My sister and I, we both decided, no way are we going to teach!" Thomas recalls. "That was hard, that was a twenty-four-seven job! Working nine to four in a bank looked good. And when I went to work at the bank? It reinforced what I'd always believed—that I had the intellectual ability and drive to succeed no matter what other people thought black people could and could not do."

The challenge initially, she reflects, was logistical: to make it all work, she put her studies at Georgia State on hold temporarily, instead investing her time in getting to know her white coworkers and managers—not by suppressing her opinions when asked, but by saying what she thought. "I had a reputation for speaking my mind," she says. "At my retirement party, that was something everybody noted: you could count on Geri to be utterly straight with you." But back then, she remarks, it was easier for black and white people to be forthright with each other. "We went to parties at each others' homes," she points out. "We invested in getting to know each other, socially and culturally. We could ask questions. We'd talk about everything, and no one felt threatened." Many of the white people she invested in getting to know back then, she says, wound up at her retirement party last year; she went to their children's weddings, and they attended her children's weddings. She just doesn't see people forging those kinds of relationships today. "There was more of a willingness, back then, to put yourself out there and be authentic," she reflects.

Her investment paid off. Thomas was promoted through a series of back-office functions and then moved into HR, where she handled recruiting and oversaw hiring for all of the bank's lines of business.

Then came the acid test. Shortly after she arrived in HR, the bank announced it was freezing all hiring, and that there would be lay-offs in each department. Thomas braced for bad news. "I was last to come in, so when they said they'd be cutting, I assumed it would be me that would be the first to go," she recalls. But when the dust settled—and despite the fact she hadn't yet finished her degree—she still had her job. For the first time, Thomas says, it occurred to her that, despite working in an environment so white she had to walk outside to see another person of color, she had career prospects. Her opinion mattered; colleagues sought her out for it ("People would ask me what I thought, and I was silly enough to believe they wanted me to tell them," she recalls. "And I would."). Three years later, when the woman for whom she'd worked in HR started reporting to her, Thomas realized what those prospects were: management.

Certainly she felt herself capable. "I often assessed my supervisors and thought, '*Seriously*?' I knew for sure I was smarter than a lot of people ahead of me. And I worked hard enough, so why wouldn't I be running things? If I'm going to do it, why wouldn't I be at the top? That's how I approached it."

And while she was under no illusion that her opportunities were equivalent to what was offered to her white peers, she saw a pathway to leadership open up for her. When Nation's Bank (later rebranded as Bank of America) took over in the nineties, Thomas was invited to be on its first diversity council. In 2002, she was appointed to run its diversity and inclusion practice, and in 2009, she became Georgia market president, a position that tasked her with driving business integration opportunities across the state as well as overseeing corporate social responsibility. No one in HR had ever been asked to take on that role, but with her ties to the greater Atlanta community— Thomas sits on the boards of Councilors of the Carter Center and the Buckhead Coalition, and serves on the Board of Directors of the Atlanta Committee for Progress, the Georgia State University Foundation, Leadership Atlanta, and the Executive Leadership Council—no one else, as her sponsor pointed out, was nearly as qualified. "He said, 'Geri, I've thought about this, I've talked with Ken Lewis, we've looked around, and you're the only person really who could be market president.'" Thomas thought about it, and agreed. "If you're going to have to do the work, you may as well have the role," she remembers her husband telling her.

Looking back on her career today, Thomas takes pride in the fact that she succeeded on the basis of who she was. "I never wanted to be viewed as not authentic," she says. "If people asked me what I thought, I'd tell them. I was bold, because I was willing to accept the consequences. Not everybody is." She reflects a moment and then adds, "I did it on my terms. And at some point, my terms were okay with everybody else."

Despite significant barriers to success, some black women pushed through to positions of national prominence. Shirley Chisholm, for example, made history when she was elected to Congress in 1968 and further demolished both racial and gender barriers when she announced her bid for presidency in 1972 under the auspices of the Feminist Party.[29] Coretta Scott King, another trailblazer, kept the memory and mission of her husband, Dr. Martin Luther King Jr., alive through her outspoken condemnation of the South African system of apartheid in the 1980s.[30] Writers Maya Angelou, Toni Morrison, and Alice Walker garnered international acclaim with their unflinching portraits of black women and men; Morrison was awarded the Nobel Prize in Literature in 1993.[31]

It is no coincidence, however, that most of the leadership gains made by black women in the past three decades have been outside the corridors of corporate America. While black women today find themselves, as Rhimes noted, far better off than they were thirty years ago in terms of access to white-collar professions, within those professions they are still confronting challenges that slow their advancement and deny them empowerment. As a result, we find they're even more stuck and stalled than white women: 17 percent of white women make it to the marzipan layer, that sticky band of management below leadership, but only 9 percent of black women do. Indeed, black women hold a mere 5 percent of managerial and professional positions, and less than 3 percent of the board seats of Fortune 500 companies.[32] And just one black woman—Xerox CEO Ursula Burns—helms a Fortune 500 company.[33] These numbers are all the more dismal in light of the fact that many Fortune 500 companies target high-potential women with initiatives aimed specifically at advancing them into leadership.

Black women's career stall stems in part from the fact that antidiscrimination measures look at race and gender separately. As we have seen, diversity initiatives and activist groups frequently target women or people of color, but not black women, who are marginalized by both groups—an approach that race theorist Kimberlé Crenshaw attributes to widespread failure to grasp the intersectionality of black women's experience.[34] "When African American women or any other women of color experience either compound or overlapping discrimination," she observes, "the law…just [is] not there to come to their defense."[35] So while Fortune 500 companies congratulate themselves on having met their diversity quota with a (still meager) 17 percent of women directors, the vast majority of those women are white.[36] As Crenshaw puts it, "Women of color are invisible in plain sight."[37]

With findings from nationally representative survey data and scores of interviews, we intend to probe this intersection, and put an end to black women's invisibility. It is our contention that feminism can only move forward for all women if first we recognize—and honor—the differences among women.

PART ONE:
WOMEN AND POWER

Women have arrived in the C-suite, but not in numbers remotely representative of their workforce participation or leadership potential. In this section we show what power looks like when women wield it, with portraits of two remarkable leaders. Then we explore how power eludes black women and white women today, for reasons that owe much to their different histories and starting gates.

1

Power in Black and White

In 2000, as a newly anointed Henry Crown Fellow, Mellody Hobson attended a week-long seminar at the Aspen Institute in Colorado. It was a heady experience, she recalls, spending each day in the mountains discussing the works of Gandhi, Hobbes, and Locke with sixteen other extremely accomplished young leaders, particularly because the seminar was moderated by Skip Battle, the retired titan of Arthur Andersen Consulting and former CEO of online search engine Ask Jeeves. "Pearls of wisdom fell from his mouth," she recalls. When the week came to a close, Battle turned to her. "Mellody, no doubt you will do good in our society," he began. "But are you willing to put yourself in harm's way?"

At thirty-one, Hobson had already done a lot of good. She was president of Ariel Investments, steering a firm with over $3.5 billion in assets under management. In her community, she served as director on the boards of the Chicago Public Library, the Library Foundation, and the Civic Federation of Chicago. She also sat on the boards of the Field Museum, the Chicago Public Education Fund, the 21st Century Charter School, the Women's Business

Development Council, Do Something, and St. Ignatius College Preparatory. And yet she knew exactly what Battle was getting at: was she daring to speak her truth, as a black woman—however uncomfortable it would make those around her? Was she capable of being that kind of leader?

In the ensuing years, Hobson seized every opportunity to speak out where she felt her truth might make a difference, using her board seats to advocate for membership to include more women and people of color, and using her platform as president of Ariel to help people grow their financial literacy. Wherever she went, whomever she was with, she elected to be "unapologetically black."

Then, in May of 2014, presented with the opportunity to command the TED stage, Hobson delivered a fourteen-minute talk called "Color Blind or Color Brave?" She talked openly about her own challenges as a person of color, and then she urged listeners to talk openly about differences.

It was undeniably a risky truth to speak. Friends and colleagues alike had told her not to do it. "People will see you as militant," they warned. "They'll typecast you, make you 'the race issue,' see you as having your fist in the air—and that will hurt Ariel." Moments before she took the TED stage in Vancouver, an exchange underscored the wisdom of their advice. A woman Hobson knew turned to her in the green room to ask what her speech was about. "Race," Hobson told her. "Grace?" the woman responded, smiling. "What a great topic!" Hobson calmly repeated herself. The woman's smile collapsed, and she looked away. "She didn't know what to say," says Hobson, recalling the tension in that room. "But I had something to say, and I was the perfect person to say it."

Today, Hobson is known for many things in addition to her stewardship of Ariel Investments: her seat at the head of the table at DreamWorks Animation; her circle of friends, which includes Sheryl Sandberg; her marriage to filmmaker George Lucas; and her daughter, Everest. Vanity Fair profiled her in 2015; TIME magazine named her one of the World's 100 Most Influential People.[38] But what Hobson is most proud of, about herself as a leader, is choosing to speak out about, and model, being color brave. Because she delivered that inconvenient truth well before Michael Brown's shooting in Ferguson, MO, and Freddie Gray's death in Baltimore, MD, Hobson forced the nation to confront its own complicity in systemic discrimination and acts of unconscious bias.

"I didn't know I was 'early,'" she says, reflecting on her speech in Vancouver. "I said my truth about needing to seek out difference, challenge our own assumptions about others, because it's worked really well for me. Some of the power I have today is related to living that truth."

Putting oneself in harm's way, she clarifies, doesn't mean stepping in front of a metaphorical bus: when a client's bias or bigotry makes her the person in the room unlikely to advance the interests of her team, she will step back to let someone else own the relationship. "There are times I know, I'm fully cognizant, that my presence may not work," she says. But living her truth means acknowledging that she will make others uncomfortable and accepting that there may be negative consequences. "I'm okay with that," she asserts. "It's as Skip said: What are you willing to stand up for? What idea, what value, will you quit for? It starts with the individual. You have to make it happen. I'm supported by some amazing people here; my environment helps me stand up for what I believe. But I hold myself accountable."

―――――――――――――

As editor-in-chief of Cosmopolitan *and an editorial director at Hearst, Joanna Coles is one of the most talked-about powerhouses in the media world. Her celebrity derives in part, certainly, from making herself highly visible on celebrity circuits. She's taken lead roles on* Project Runway, *dispensing fashion advice in place of Tim Gunn. She's joined Mika Brzezinski on* Morning Joe *to discuss executive presence as well as to kick off New York's Fashion Week, where she was photographed alongside the runway, chatting up Miley Cyrus. In her platinum pixie cut, stiletto heels, and chic designer sheaths, Joanna Coles is as much a fashion doyenne as she is a media titan.*

But Coles continues to make headlines because she has taken the most widely read women's magazine in the world and used it as a platform to elevate women's issues as they dominate politics, social policy, business, and the workplace. If under Helen Gurley Brown Cosmo's *mandate was to empower women in the bedroom, under Coles that mandate has expanded to empowering women in the boardroom, as well. She recruited Sheryl Sandberg to oversee and launch the magazine's first-ever career guide, focusing on financial advice because Coles believes that nothing is more liberating for women than having the know-how to attain financial independence. She's reallocated resources to do serious investigative reporting, offering readers insight on everything from how to press charges when raped to how to choose the most effective birth control.[39] Painstakingly professional coverage of controversial topics has gotten* Cosmo *nominated, in turn, for prestigious industry awards; in 2014,* Cosmo *picked up its first-ever National Magazine Award, and in 2015, it made finalist for Magazine of the Year.[40] Advertisers have taken notice: the September 2013 issue set a record in the magazine's 128-year history. Readership at* Cosmo, *with one hundred million readers in more than one hundred countries worldwide, is also at an all-time high.*

Coles's business savvy and breathless schedule—this is a woman whose desk is positioned above a treadmill—have made her the subject of countless articles, from a New York Times *glimpse of her home life (she's married to screenwriter and human rights activist Peter Godwin, with whom she has two sons) to a* Fast Company *recounting of how she ascended to Hearst's highest office. But what Coles wants to stress is how much she relishes the voice that her visibility and media platform afford her.*

"I didn't realize before I became editor-in-chief how much I was going to enjoy being in charge," she says. "I've been so exhilarated creating direction for this magazine, seeing my ideas of what a magazine for women should be and watching it take shape over a number of issues—it's thrilling. Of course it requires a lot of other people; I'm not doing this on my own. But I'm the person making the decisions. It's my vision I'm putting out there. And it's absolutely fabulous."

To look at women like Hobson and Coles, one might conclude that, despite their different starting gates, black women and white have finally arrived.

These women are not simply lining corridors of corporate America, lending support to those in power. Rather, they occupy the C-suite's corner office. They're at the top of their respective professions, widely recognized for their achievement, amply rewarded for their acumen. Each has embraced leadership, shouldering its responsibilities both on the job and outside in the wider community. Each has enjoyed career success that has enriched, rather than impoverished, her personal life. And each has chosen to wield her power for good, driving change for an entire generation of women both black and white.

In many ways, they embody the feminist ideal. They exercise ably all of the choices that women before them fought hard for decades to bestow.

But our research reveals that they are also, lamentably, the exception among exceptional women. Ambitious, capable women today do not inhabit the C-suite in numbers anywhere near parity with ambitious, capable men: women constitute a mere 4.6 percent of Fortune 500 CEOs; only 14.6 percent hold executive officer positions.[41] Black women in particular are absent from the upper echelons of the private sector, as noted in our Introduction. At this writing, only one of the twenty-two women at the helms of Fortune 500 companies is black, and only two black women—Mellody Hobson and Ursula Burns—serve as chief executives of publicly traded companies.[42]

Power eludes black women and white women today, we find, for reasons that owe much to their different histories and starting gates.

BLACK WOMEN WANT POWER

Our data reveals black women to be nearly three times as likely as white (22 percent vs. 8 percent) to aspire to a powerful position with a prestigious title. Black women today draw strength and inspiration from a long line of matriarchs: women who prevailed as breadwinners, heads of household, and leaders in their churches, schools, and communities despite a relentless undertow of discrimination and economic hardship. "Our mothers had power, our grandmothers had power, we see what it can do," says Ella Bell, founder and president of ASCENT: Leading Multicultural Women to the Top (a leadership development program), as well as an associate professor of Business Administration at the Tuck School of Business at Dartmouth College. "The reality is, the way we view gender, as it intersects with race and class—and you can't look at it otherwise—gives us our understanding of who we are as women," says Bell, whose book, *Our Separate Ways*, maps the personal and professional journeys of dozens of women in both communities. "As a result, what it means to be a woman, a feminist, in the black community is very different from what it means to be a woman in the white community. Rosa Parks is part of my lineage. Because black mothers raise their daughters to understand the shoulders we stand on, we have a different sense of who we are, what we can take on, and what we can survive."

Part of black women's interest in private-sector power can be explained by the fact that their mothers and grandmothers simply did not have access to it. As Geri Thomas points out, "you knew black women could be in charge. They ran schools, they were head nurses—in black schools and black hospitals." Thomas's mother was one of them: she had a college degree, but no opportunities to exercise it outside of education or nursing. "My mother had to be a teacher," Thomas says. "That was all you could be, then. So my sister and I, we were going to grab ambition by the horns."

With increased access to higher education in the seventies, says Bell, black women attained degrees in fields where their authority was guaranteed: in medicine, law, education, and accounting. Legally, with the passage of the Civil Rights Act of 1964, black women had to be provided equal access to employment opportunities across all industry sectors.[43] "But just because the law said so didn't mean behavior followed," explains Thomas. Consciously or unconsciously, black women favored employment where they could be assured of job security. "We talked about getting hired by the private sector," recalls Charlene Drew Jarvis, "but we also knew you could be terminated at any time for any reason. I remember thinking, 'I never want to be subjected to that kind of uncertainty or unfairness.' I did not want to be at the mercy of some white guy who had no respect for my intellect, or my contribution; who saw me as somebody who counts pencils. I wanted more control than that."

Perhaps that explains why black women's representation in the ranks of corporate America is a relatively recent phenomenon. According to talent specialists and corporate educators, they come with clear goals and intense commitment to achieving them. "They know what they want to do, and how they want to do it," says Bell, who runs leadership development programs for women at several multinational companies. "The level of confidence you see in these women is because, compared to a generation ago, they have a better understanding of expectations, assumptions, and opportunities. They're not afraid to bring more of themselves to the table, to share who they are and make known their experiences and perspectives."

PORTRAITS IN POWER: MELISSA JAMES

As early as high school, Melissa James, managing director and global head of loan products at Morgan Stanley, knew she wanted a career in business. By her sophomore year of college, she knew she wanted to go into finance. "Earning well was part of it," she says.

But not because she'd grown up poor: quite the contrary. James came from a privileged household. Her father, a physician, had attended medical school in Switzerland; her mother had graduated from Fisk, a historically black college, before earning a PhD in anatomy and physiology from the University of Chicago. Even her grandparents (on her father's side) had college degrees. James was enrolled in a private elementary school; she leveraged a specialized high school experience at Stuyvesant High School, a magnet school, to get into Yale University, and obtained an MBA from Harvard University.

But because she lived in the inner-city community where her father served mostly black patients, ranging from the working poor to the middle class, James was keenly aware of the disparities which existed between different socioeconomic classes. "Because many blacks didn't have the economic safety net of their white counterparts, I learned early how important it was to be master of your own destiny," says James. "I saw the value of entrepreneurship: that to accumulate real wealth, you needed to own and control the means of production. That is what I was in pursuit of."

James also liked telling other people what to do. "I was bossy as a kid, and business was a place to be bossy," she observes, laughing. Yet what hooked her when she got to Wall Street was finding that she'd landed among her own: "smart people with backgrounds like mine, liberal arts majors who were similar to my undergrad peers at Yale." She loved working alongside bright, highly motivated, performance-oriented people. "You can make the world a better place by being in finance, but that's not the only thing that drew me," she says. "I saw myself being empowered, and being in a position to empower others."

Today, James is one of the 75 Most Powerful Blacks on Wall Street.[44] She oversees $70 billion in loan commitments, a business she helped establish for Morgan Stanley. She's overseen many of the firm's lucrative endeavors, particularly in debt capital markets, where she helped raise billions in capital for corporate clients. She's also had a hand in the firm's most complex transactions with General Electric Capital Corporation, DuPont, and Agere.

"I have to pinch myself sometimes," says James, "because I'm living my dream. This is the vision I had for myself, and with the help from others along the way I've been able to live it and am very grateful."

Our data echoes Bell's observation about confidence: black women we surveyed are 25 percent more likely than white women to have both clear near-term (50 percent vs. 40 percent) and long-term (40 percent vs. 32 percent) career goals. They are also considerably more likely than white women (43 percent vs. 30 percent) to be confident that they can succeed in a position of power.

So it is all the more surprising, and dismaying, that despite their confidence, their ambition, and their credentials, many qualified black women fail to get traction on the steep road to the top—a situation alarmingly similar to the one that Geri Thomas described upon entering the white-collar professional workforce in 1970.

AMBITIOUS, BUT AMBIVALENT

White women are more conflicted about pursuing and wielding power. They hunger for influence, we find, but believe they can have influence without the platform of formally recognized leadership. Leadership scares them. Asked whether they would accept an executive leadership position if it were offered tomorrow, 36 percent said no; 43 percent said they would accept it with reservations.

To be sure, both black and white women are aware that leadership will impose some heavy demands. Some 56 percent of white women and 52 percent of black women believe the burdens of leadership outweigh the rewards. Among the negatives that factor into their calculus is the fear that they will have *no* control over their schedule: 67 percent of white and 65 percent of black women say that needing to be available "anytime, anywhere" does not appeal to them when considering executive leadership positions.

The difference is, black women push ahead in their careers regardless of concerns about balancing all responsibilities. They're clear-eyed about the burdens; they're just not conflicted about wanting power. Whereas white women, having assessed the burdens, grow ambivalent—and rein in their ambition.

Such ambivalence toward power seems likewise rooted in history. White women today struggle to shed the burden of gender-role expectations attendant on their socioeconomic privilege—privilege that for centuries situated white women outside the paid labor force as homemakers and helpmates. The domestic roles that Friedan found so oppressive in 1968 continue to constrict them: acquiring new roles in the workforce hasn't relieved them of the roles assigned at birth, but rather pitched them into an impossible bind where excelling at one means perforce failing at the other. The work-life conflict hasn't abated for white women, despite declining birthrates and mounting wage-earning pressures. A stunning 35 percent of white women age forty and over in our sample do not have children. Fully 61 percent of white women in our sample that are married or living with a partner earn at least as much as their partners or spouses do. And yet white professional women, despite their fierce ambition (some 81 percent consider themselves ambitious), appear ambitious for something other than power. Despite the fact that we see young women starting out their careers intent on attaining positions of upper management, this intent is not matched by their older counterparts. White women between the ages of twenty-one and thirty-four are twice as likely as white women between the ages of thirty-five and fifty to say they aspire to a powerful position with a prestigious title.

And thus we see, half a century after women marched on Washington demanding equal rights, men and women with equal leadership potential arriving at starkly different destinations mid- to late-career. Men arrive in the executive suite, while qualified women continue to tour middle management. The numbers tell the story: women in the US hold less than 15 percent of Fortune 500 executive positions.[45]

This skewed outcome, as talent specialists well know, exacts an insupportable toll on both women and the companies that employ them. Women who have invested in their education and professional development—such as the 36 percent of US women and 32 percent of UK women on course to acquire an MBA or industry-relevant tertiary degree—fail to reap the dividends in terms of fulfilled potential or lucrative position.[46] Employers that have invested considerable sums developing women for leadership roles are in danger of seeing their investment go out the door, possibly never to return, or failing to deliver anticipated returns in the form of a more diversified C-suite or boardroom. Companies whose leadership remains homogeneous, as the Center for Talent Innovation (CTI)'s 2013 innovation research shows, lose a critical competitive edge: they're less likely to elicit market-worthy ideas, less likely to green-light them, and less likely to increase market share or grow their global footprint.[47]

Thus we find ourselves at an impasse unimaginable to our feminist forebears: exceptional women stand at the threshold to power either because they're not invited to cross it or because they're afraid to. What is to be done? How might white women come to embrace leadership as the means to liberation? How might black women shrug off the mantle of invisibility that keeps them from claiming the roles they're prepared to fill?

In the next section, we'll explore what exactly is holding women back and, having exposed those tripwires, map ways for women to leap over them.

PART TWO:
THE BATTLE BEFORE US

White women and black confront different challenges as they strive to advance in the white-collar workplace—challenges that derive from their different histories and conceptions of workplace equality. For black women, invisibility denies them the advocacy and backing they need to break out of middle management. For white women, ambivalence toward power acts as a brake. For all women, however, forward progress depends on cultivating sponsors: leaders who will create opportunities for them to shine and keep them on track to fulfill their leadership potential.

2

Black Women Are Invisible

At the close of 2014, Lorraine,* a regional director at a medical device manufacturer with twenty years of experience supervising her firm's top accounts, approached her boss to talk about the opportunities he saw for her in 2015. It wasn't that she was unhappy, she explained: she took pride in her work, in the relationships she'd built, and in the value she delivered. But she'd been in her current role for six years, and hungered for new opportunities to grow and learn. She'd watched as her peers took on assignments that put them on track for profit-and-loss positions with strategic oversight. She wanted that responsibility; her track record, she pointed out, was impeccable in terms of leading teams to exceed revenue targets. She wanted to be put in charge of a business unit and report directly to the CEO. And if that was not in the cards, she wanted to know what the firm had in mind for her—which succession plan she fit into.

Her boss heard her out, and then said, "Lorraine, you've reached a milestone you probably never

* Indicates name change to ensure source's anonymity, here and throughout the text.

imagined. You're among the top two percent of people here who make over two hundred thousand dollars a year. Do we really need to talk about what you haven't yet achieved? The milestones you haven't met?"

The meeting was clearly over. Lorraine forced a smile to her lips, thanked him for his time, and retreated to her desk shaking with suppressed fury. "I was beside myself," she admits, recollecting the exchange. "Would he have said such a thing to a man? Why is it, when you ask for things as a black woman, you're made to feel you should apologize for asking?"

Lorraine has given herself a time frame: if in six months she hasn't been given a stretch assignment or other growth opportunity, she's going to leave the firm. "I would be interested in running a small company," she confides. "I've got the track record; I just need to get over my doubts."

At the same time, however, she's dismayed at the prospect of having to leave a company where she's built a significant book of business and proven her leadership skills. "I've seen this company take a risk on certain people—some white women, some black men— because maybe they will work out," she reflects. "So why not me? I know they're comfortable with what I do and how I do it. Why not give *me* a chance? What have I been proving for the last twenty years, if not that I can be relied on to help grow this company?"

STUCK AND STALLED

In corporate America, black women hammer at the glass ceiling, but rarely break through. Despite their fierce ambition (91 percent consider themselves ambitious), black women are more likely than white to say they feel stalled in their careers (44 percent vs. 30 percent). Less than half (45 percent) are satisfied with their rate of advancement. They stick firmly in the marzipan layer right below top management—if they even reach it—in sight of the C-suite but seemingly not in the sights of those who occupy it.

Why? Why, as Lorraine asks, aren't qualified black women given a chance to run the company?

CONSCIOUS AND UNCONSCIOUS BIAS

We cannot overlook, among the myriad reasons our research uncovers, the role that bias plays. Unconscious bias—or even conscious bias—tortures the career path of both black and white women, from the very first step. A job opening may not be shared with them; their application may receive less attention based on their gender alone; their qualifications may be assessed absent objective guidelines; their skills may be deemed appropriate for only limited job functions; their performance may be assessed on an unlevel playing field, where they've been given the most difficult clients or least likely sales prospects. While multinationals proclaim and enforce rigorous antidiscrimination policies, bias persists at all levels, because rarely is it overt enough to be deemed outright discrimination.

That's true for all women. But black women experience bias for both reasons of gender and race. To those in power (overwhelmingly, white men), black women are particularly invisible.

One executive and business advisor offers an example. At the consultancy where she used to work, she watched her boss repeatedly offer the lead role on new business to a colleague of hers—a white male whom she had hired to help her execute a massive cost reduction project for a multimillion-dollar client. "My boss simply couldn't remember that it was my leadership, my work, and not that of the guy I'd hired and promoted while I was doing it," she says. "He'd look me straight in the eye and say, 'Why don't we put Tom on this new account? He did such a great job with that cost reduction project.'"

One senior vice president and executive editor at a big cable network likewise describes a phenomenon that occurred with some frequency early in her career as a broadcast journalist—before she had won the backing of powerful leaders at the news channel. "During editorial meetings in the early nineties," she recalls, "I noticed that sometimes if I were to say, 'Let's do A,' the room would continue in its discussion. I'd hear that idea of mine coming out of someone else's mouth. And then the room would hear it, understand it, and get behind it." She adds, "Initially I thought it was race related.

Then I began to think it was not only race related but also gender related."

Even when black women insist that leaders acknowledge their contribution, recognition doesn't necessarily translate into opportunity. "I feel like I'm always the bridesmaid, never the bride," says Nichelle,* a twenty-year veteran of her firm. "My performance reviews have been uniformly outstanding: I could run every one of our leadership programs, and my exposure to leaders is crafted very strategically. But despite being supported, I'm not promoted." She adds, "This leaves me to surmise that the only things preventing my advancement are my color, size, and shape. I don't know what's said about me behind closed doors, but I look around and see that the females who get the promotions are usually white and regardless of race, are almost always cute and petite. And I have to wonder, as a big girl over fifty, what my chances here really are."

Such entrenched bias helps explain why 43 percent of black women say that senior leaders at their firm are not capable of seeing their leadership potential—a dismaying number, one that we might have imagined being true in 1976 but not in 2016. Nearly one in three (32 percent) black women believe that a person of color would never get a top position at her firm, no matter how able or high-performing—another statistic that seems more appropriate to our mothers' generation.[48] Some 37 percent of black women we surveyed say they don't feel comfortable speaking out about experiences of bias or discrimination. One interviewee said she was uncomfortable to do so in case it would "fan the flames of the angry-black-woman stereotype" and further compromise black women's chances at promotion.

Indeed, calling out bias is a tricky business. Patrice,* a financial analyst, describes one instance early in her career when she alerted a manager to what she felt was discriminatory treatment. "I'd been doing the work of the role I'd been promised, but had yet to receive the title and pay associated with that promotion," she explains. When the manager took no action, she took her complaint to the head of HR. At twenty-five years old, it was "scary," she says, to issue an ultimatum, and wind up at headquarters flanked by HR. Some coworkers insinuated she was too full of herself. "I did what was right for me in my career and I expected to be compensated for the position." For about three months she endured a "really uncomfortable, really messy" work environment. "But I'd be damned if I let this happen again, this failure to recognize my ability and reward it," she says.

So black women grapple with a catch-22. If they don't speak out, they remain invisible, and easily passed over for stretch assignments, high-visibility projects, and promotion; if they cry foul, they get tagged as a liability to be wary of, an angry black woman who might levy a lawsuit on her employer, rather than as an asset to cultivate and prize for her complementary networks and market insights.

VISIBLE, BUT SILENT

Compounding black women's invisibility to senior leaders who might back them for promotion is their inclination to "put their head down"—as Denise Diallo, a partner with global law firm White & Case LLP in its Global Banking Practice puts it—and "make no noise," working even harder, in the expectation (or hope) that their work will speak for them.

CTI's extensive research on sponsorship documents this tendency among white women as well—what we dubbed the Tiara Syndrome, as it describes the unspoken expectation among ambitious women that if they outperform others or exceed targets, a leader will simply feel obliged to crown them with a promotion. They won't need to speak out, because their work stands out.

The legacy of affirmative action makes this tendency even more pronounced among black women, who fervently wish to have promotions be awarded irrespective of factors like race and gender. They want to shine without affirmative-action considerations tarnishing their accomplishment. They want to stand out, our interviewees clarify, not because they're black but because they provide incredible value.

That is naïve and wishful thinking, says Diallo; black women have to call attention to the value they add and demand they be given the opportunities they've earned. "What they don't realize," she explains, "is that it's not enough to deliver two hundred percent on the deal. You must also be recognized as the person who's listed alongside the partners even though you're not yet one of them. You've got to be introduced actively to clients, and pushed or promoted to play a role in certain firm activities. You cannot be the one trailing behind a partner, holding the bags; you cannot let anyone wonder why you're there."

In other ways, too, black women fail to call attention to experience that would get them tapped for professional development or for high-potential initiatives. Talent officers tell us, for example, that black women are reticent to mention their considerable commitment to institutions and organizations outside of work—involvement that gives them leadership skills and experience as well as a powerful network. As we documented in our 2005 *Leadership in Our Midst* study, that reticence is born of the fear that making known the extent of their external commitments to managers will make them look less committed or less available to their employer. But silence on this front is something black women simply can't afford, says Valerie Grillo, the former chief diversity officer and current VP and HR business partner for the US consumer products and services unit at American Express. "Black women will talk to me in passing about their board involvement, or mention they spent the weekend with the Girl Scout troop they lead," she says. "I have to stop them and ask, 'Does your leader know about that?' Because they don't perceive the value of sharing this: they don't realize that the community work they're doing gives them experience and exposure and additional skills that translate back to the office."

Or perhaps, as Geri Thomas, the recently retired chief diversity officer at Bank of America, suggests, black women aren't so much reticent to talk about their external roles as they are unaware of how to leverage them internally. Thomas attributes much of her own career success to her ability to make her leadership outside of the bank—and her access to other community leaders in Atlanta—a marketable asset. "I'm a native here," she says, "and all of us who are in business and in nonprofit leadership know each other because we work on the same things. I made sure people at Bank of America knew that, and understood the access I had as a leader in my city. So that when it came time to name a market president, someone to represent the bank—someone who everybody knows and respects—I was their clear choice."

A SHORTFALL OF SPONSORS

Successful black women, our interviews make clear, have one thing in common: a powerful person, somewhere along the way, has lent them critical career traction by providing stretch assignments, talking them up behind closed doors, and pushing for their promotion. Every senior black female executive we interviewed has had wonderful mentors, too, of course. But each attributes her success to a sponsor, someone who, as one put it, "initiates action on your behalf, often without your knowledge." Marianne,* an AVP in market development at a telecommunications firm, credits her network of diverse supporters, including a white male manager, with not only her promotions but also her rehiring after an absence from the company. Angela Daker, the only female and only black partner in White & Case's Miami office, attributes her success to "a broad range of support" that she cultivated over the years by doggedly seeking commonality and forging relationships with people ostensibly unlike herself but who were in a position to see how she engaged with clients and delivered on projects. "I always understood that, if I had the right relationships and support, I'd have a chance," she says.

But Moore and Daker are among the scant 11 percent of black women within the US who win sponsorship.[49] Black women stick out like unicorns in corporate America, and yet as one senior leader observes, people in power tend only to see, get to know, and come to trust, people like themselves. Compounding that problem, we find, is the fact that many executives of color, insecure about their own relationship capital in a majority hierarchy, hesitate to sponsor minorities.[50]

Thus it would appear that black women who are ready to lead cannot get traction because they remain invisible to those whose advocacy they need in order to break through to leadership roles. Without sponsors, or leaders who believe in their leadership potential, they don't get the plum assignments; they are not assigned to high-visibility projects; they are not entrusted with key client relationships; they are not tapped for professional development or high-potential initiatives; and their name doesn't come up when succession planners confer behind closed doors. Decades of discrimination can make them reticent, moreover, to assert their value, claim credit for their accomplishments, or leverage their external leadership roles. By remaining silent on top of being invisible, black women widen the chasm between themselves and potential sponsors, foreclosing advocacy that leaders may well be poised to offer if only they were made aware of the value these women could bring.

And so leadership remains disproportionately white and male, signaling to black women that someone who looks like them will never attain a top job. A shortfall of sponsorship culminates in a dearth of role models, which demoralizes black women in the ranks and undercuts efforts to recruit minority professionals, driving further downward the spiral of black representation at much of the Fortune 1000.

There are no easy answers and no easy fixes for this vicious cycle. In many ways, the onus is on leadership, and not black women, to take corrective measures. Still, there are pathways to sponsorship that black women might better exploit. We will map these in Chapter Four.

3

Ambition and Ambivalence

With twelve years' worth of data on professional women, we know that women are not only ambitious: we know what they are ambitious *for*. Women want five things from work.

First and foremost, we find, they want to be able to flourish: to work at jobs that allow them to self-actualize. Next, women want to be able to excel: to be challenged in what they know and do precisely because in rising above that challenge they will have proven something important both to themselves and to others. Third on the list: women want work to grant them a sense of meaning and purpose. They want desperately to make a positive difference in other people's lives, not merely in their company's bottom line. Number Four: women wish to empower others, and *be* empowered by others. They seek senior colleagues who are willing to take a bet on them and advocate for their next big opportunity; they also seek high-achieving junior colleagues who deepen their bench, extend their reach, and burnish their brand. And last but not at all least, women want to earn well. They aspire to be financially secure and independent, and to provide a comfortable lifestyle for themselves, their offspring, and their parents.

Across ethnicity and age, we find remarkable consensus among women in terms of their five priorities. Black women want these five things just as fervently as white women; women at the outset of their career are as inclined as women in the prime of their working lives to identify these five things. Black women are more likely to value earning well than white women: they are 50 percent more likely (81 percent vs. 54 percent) to say this is important in their careers. They are also more likely than white women to cite financial independence as one of their top three goals.

But as we pointed out in Chapter One, black women are more likely than white to see power at work as the means to getting everything they want from life. White women, in contrast, are more likely than black women to harbor very low expectations of a top job. For example, while most white women do expect that, as executives, they'll be able to excel and earn well, very few (15 percent) believe that an executive position will enable them to empower others or be empowered (compared to 26 percent of black women). And few (16 percent) imagine that, in a top job, they will flourish, compared to 28 percent of black women.

The reality of a top job, as described by women in power of all races, is altogether different from the expectation: Nearly two out of three (63 percent) women who have power report that they indeed have meaning and purpose at work. A robust 61 percent say they are empowered and in a position to empower others. More than half of this group (58 percent) say they're flourishing, and the vast majority (87 percent) say work enables them to excel. The only area where women's expectation of a top job actually exceeds reality is with regard to compensation: although 73 percent of women expected a top job would compensate them well, only 37 percent of those with power say they earn well.

These low expectations inform, not surprisingly, white women's appetite for executive leadership. A mere 8 percent (as compared to 22 percent of black women) say they aspire to a powerful position with a prestigious title. That's a statistic backed up by a raft of testimony we've gathered from interviews and focus groups with white women over the years. "I could be CFO if I wanted to," one senior exec told us. "But I don't want to. The job I have is more interesting." Another woman explained that she had worked hard to achieve balance in her life, and wasn't eager to take on a position—i.e. one with profit-and-loss responsibility—that might destroy it. "I'm perfectly happy where I am," she said. More than a third of female senior vice presidents (36 percent) we surveyed in 2010 admitted they didn't want to get promoted. "My next promotion would be to a country manager position," one senior VP told us. "The job itself is appealing but there are too many drawbacks for my kids."

THE CONFIDENCE GAP

Other researchers who have likewise noted women's hesitation to pursue a top job or stretch opportunity posit that women (*all* women, as these studies rarely disaggregate their cohort by race) may be hardwired for self-doubt. A 2011 study conducted by the UK-based Institute of Leadership & Management found that female managers (ethnicity wasn't specified) had lower career confidence than male managers across all age groups, with 70 percent of men having high to quite-high levels of self-confidence, compared to 50 percent of women; indeed, 41 percent of women and a mere 25 percent of men said "I feel fairly self-confident but do suffer doubts about myself as well." High-confidence male managers were more likely than high-confidence female managers, moreover, to have high expectations of attaining leadership roles (67 percent of men vs. 59 percent of women). Male managers were more willing than female managers, as well, to put themselves forward for roles for which they weren't fully qualified: 20 percent of men, versus 14 percent of women, said they would apply for a job or promotion whose criteria they did not fully meet. Fully 85 percent of female managers, that is, hesitated to reach for a stretch role— making themselves less visible, the study concludes, and more likely to miss out on the opportunities and experiences necessary to make it to the top.[51]

Our own statistics affirm this hesitation, not just among white women but also among black. While

22 percent of black women say they want a powerful position with a prestigious title, that's still an astounding 78 percent who do not. And while we find black women are far more likely than white to be confident that they can succeed in a position of power (43 percent vs. 30 percent), the fact that 57 percent do not express that confidence suggests that doubt afflicts black women as well as white.

It bears emphasizing that researchers do not attribute women's low confidence to lesser ability. In 2011, cognitive scientist Zachary Estes conducted four experiments on men and women using the Mental Rotations Test, a measure of cognitive ability where men typically outscore women. In each experiment, he found he could eliminate all gender differences when he controlled for or manipulated confidence in his subjects.[52] The implication, as journalists Katty Kay and Claire Shipman note in their 2014 book *The Confidence Code,* is that self-assurance (or lack thereof) accounts for what others may assume in women to be a lack of ambition or interest in leadership. "The confidence gap is an additional lens through which to consider why it is women don't lean in," they write. "Even when we are prepared to tolerate the personal disruption that comes with aiming high, even when we have plenty of ambition, we fundamentally doubt ourselves."[53]

Interestingly, even white women who feel confident about wielding power own up to an aversion to the heightened visibility and public scrutiny that a top job brings. Interviews that Patricia Sellers conducted in 2003 with female CEOs of Fortune 500 firms reveal that distaste. Marge Magner, then number five on Fortune's Most Powerful Women list, told Sellers that she perceived her promotion to run Citi's Global Consumer Group as "a double-edged sword" because, she said, "I'm on the front line. I have people knowing who I am—all this stuff I've avoided until now." Most of the women on Sellers's list of fifty, moreover, did not want to trade places with Carly Fiorina, CEO (then) of Hewlett-Packard and number one on the list. [54] They had no appetite for a role that invited continual media attention and public speculation about matters they deemed to be highly personal.

Lift the lid on women's ambivalence, that is, and you will find a complex stew of emotions: self-doubt, fear of failure, dislike of public scrutiny, an aversion to disruption, and fear of letting down their families.

And you won't have to look far to see who is keeping this stew asimmer.

THE CONVERSATION

In her 2012 article for *The Atlantic*, "Why Women Still Can't Have It All," Anne-Marie Slaughter, president and CEO of the New America Foundation and former dean of Princeton University's Woodrow Wilson School of Public and International Affairs, made a poignant case for revisiting the assumption that women could be effective on the job while also being a supportive partner and attentive mother. In some thirteen thousand words she catalogued the ordeal of fulfilling her responsibilities as director of policy planning for the US State Department under then-Secretary of State Hillary Clinton.[55] A grueling schedule compounded by a long-distance commute kept her from attending to her fourteen-year-old's emotional needs, contributing to her eventual realization that Super Woman was an illusion she'd been sold that simply did not deliver for thousands of working women.

Slaughter hit a nerve. In the first four days following publication, her diatribe attracted some 725 thousand unique readers, making it one of the most popular articles ever published in *The Atlantic*, and had been recommended 119 thousand times on Facebook, making it the most "liked" piece ever to appear in any version of the magazine.[56] Overnight, it brought Slaughter to prominence not as a Princeton professor, political scientist, or Obama administration policy maker, but rather as a feminist who had come to disavow the creed. Slaughter indicted working motherhood, absent systems of support from both private and public sectors, as uniquely oppressive—a point made by many a feminist before her, but always made in order to condemn the private and public sectors for withholding formalized support. Slaughter, in contrast, was also condemning feminists for misleading high-achieving women like herself to believe that wielding power equal to that of men needn't come at catastrophic cost.

No one would contest that holding a top job is a high-wire act. High-flying men and women alike confess, in our interviews, to making sacrifices and compromises. The joy and satisfaction they derive, however—as evidenced by our own data—suggests that with power, ambitious men and women get to choose the sacrifices or compromises they make. Women with power are more likely to have the five things they most want, probably because they attain the control they need to strike the balance that works for them. They're in a position to delegate. They're in charge of their calendars and can ask others to align work around their schedules. Work may need to get done, but they decide which work takes priority and how best to get it done. Feeling victimized by work is a story we'd expect to hear from women in middle management or in the early years of their careers—women who hadn't yet the autonomy so critical to achieving work-life balance. It is not the story we'd expect to hear from a State Department policymaker who led a team at the White House.

But Slaughter is by no means alone, among female leaders, in portraying leadership as a form of oppression. Think about it: female leaders tend to make headlines only if and when they are willing to speak about their work-life balance—or lack thereof. When PepsiCo CEO Indra Nooyi spoke at the Aspen Ideas Festival in July 2014, what went viral was not her ideas on how to steer a company valued at $145 billion, but rather her response to *Atlantic* editor David Bradley when he asked her to weigh in on Slaughter's article. "I think Anne-Marie's onto something," Nooyi told him. "I don't think women can have it all. I just don't think so…we *pretend* we have it all. We pretend we can have it all." She then proceeded to share her anguish about being a less-than-ideal mother and spouse. "You have to cope," she told listeners, "because you die with guilt. You just die with guilt."[57]

Ambitious women might conclude from this sort of exchange that other women won't relate to them unless they opine about the sacrifices and compromises. Even hard-chargers like Arianna Huffington, who manifestly love their extreme jobs, succumb to griping about them when their own achievement introduces the possibility of being seen as "unrelatable." She describes, in her book *Thrive*, how a chronic lack of sleep impaired her decision-making and robbed her of joy both at home and at work; in fact, much of the book is spent quantifying the tolls levied rather than the agency won by her zealous commitment to *The Huffington Post*. To hear Huffington tell it, few of us at the pinnacles of our careers are actually thriving. Her book is not a paean to self-actualization, but rather a manifesto on the health benefits of less work and more rest, meditation, and exercise.[58]

This conversation doesn't resonate with a lot of black women. To hear our interviewees tell it, "whether or not women can have it all" speaks to choices that, historically, they haven't been given. It underscores, for our black interviewees, the chasm between white and black feminists and white and black notions of liberation. "It's a conversation based on the assumption," one black telecommunications AVP told us, "that we women already hold power and can't handle it. Well, most of us don't hold power. And the black women who do? You don't hear them complain. Oprah, Michelle, Beyoncé? You don't hear them complain."

Not all white women approach leadership with ambivalence; not all black women are without conflicting emotions. But for those women whose perception of power inhibits their pursuit of it, the solution would seem fairly straightforward. Those in power need to change how they talk about wielding it, and help women see, through direct exposure early in their career, how a leadership role can amplify their agency, impact, and autonomy.

WHAT COMPANIES CAN DO

Ellen,* a manager for a telecommunications firm, is a prime example of how companies can help propel their most promising women into executive roles.

Throughout her eighteen-year career, Ellen has always seen herself as a strong contributor and capable manager. In her client-facing business, she supported tech and network operations, a role that required not only consultative competencies but also teaching and development skills. She derived considerable satisfaction working with her reports, particularly when she felt she'd gotten everything under control. "To get it balanced quite well and feel I'm contributing, and to be satisfied with our results—that was my idea of success," she says.

To hang onto that balance, she resisted taking more senior leadership roles. "Getting good positive feedback from clients, seeing your team members grow—it feeds your soul," she says. "It's hard to give that up and have to go prove yourself again in a new position." She worried, too, about imposing additional burdens on her husband, who had been with her for five of the eleven moves she'd made for her multinational employer. He was okay with her being the primary breadwinner, but an executive position, she knew, would demand of her more travel, more evening hours, more interruptions on vacation—and she feared putting that additional strain on her marriage.

In the past year, however, her feelings about holding a top job have radically changed, catalyzed in part by a leadership program in which she works with other high-potential women to solve challenges for top executives. Bolstered by her peers and encouraged by her boss, Ellen took on a new role in 2014 that has her setting strategy for fifty-two thousand people worldwide. While initially overwhelmed, she's been leveraging her network to get the answers and guidance she needs, and has learned to act through others. "I've come to see that what made me relevant in the past won't be what makes me relevant in the future," she observes.

And the future truly excites her. Her current responsibilities, coupled with the sponsorship of her boss, have put her on track for an officer's position, a role she sees within her capabilities now that she's interacting daily with other executives. Though it would make significant demands on her time, Ellen feels that by applying her newfound leadership skill sets she could successfully recalibrate her work-life balance. The plusses of power, she says, would more than compensate for the minuses. "The difference I see between where I am and where I'd be is my impact on strategy," she observes. "I'd be helping create a culture that impacts all employees in the company, not just now but in the future. I'd be growing, and contributing, in new ways."

In the last two years, that is, Ellen has come to see leadership fulfilling her life goals rather than thwarting them. Her quest for work that gives her a sense of meaning and purpose is particularly motivating. "I need to see that my contribution changes something for the betterment of others," she says. "*That's* what has me considering the move up to an officer's position in the firm."

She adds, "I only wish I'd had this leadership experience earlier in my career. Instead of taking eighteen years for me to advance, it would have taken me ten."

Ellen's story underscores our inference that women's attitude towards power and a top job is often a function of what they know and how much of an accurate picture they have of the job's demands—and of what the returns will be.

By her own admission, Ellen's perceptions of leadership were inaccurate—a function of inadequate information, an absence of ongoing support, and a dearth of positive role models (an erroneous picture not readily corrected by media portrayals of female leaders). She didn't understand that a leadership position would require a different skill set, that it wouldn't be an amped-up version of her managerial role, but rather a whole new way of getting things done through (and with) other people. She didn't appreciate what power would give her, in terms of her ability to make a measurable difference. She expected her relationships at work and at home would suffer. And she expected she'd see her ethical and personal values compromised.

These expectations blinded her to the paradoxical truth about leadership: with power comes added responsibility, but also liberation from the tyranny of being subordinate to other people's schedules and agendas. "Junior women operate in one environment, with one set of resources, within a narrowly defined role," observes Valerie Grillo of American Express. "They don't realize, you can't use the criteria based on your current experience to judge what's ahead. The higher you ascend, the more influence you have across the organization, and the more resources you have at your disposal to get things done. With power, women can create the work-life balance they're so desperately seeking."

PROGRAM EXPOSURE TO LEADERSHIP

Companies can utterly transform women's perceptions of executive roles by exposing them, as Ellen was exposed, to leadership in action. AT&T's Executive Women's Leadership Experience, for example, gives twenty high-potential women exposure to senior executives while teaching them about the strategy of the company and how to become successful leaders. The program consists of a curriculum of three sessions that build on one another, starting with a focus on the company's strategy, its vision for the future, and its brand. Next, participants break down the company's business model, learn about technical relevancy and good negotiation techniques, and engage in discussions with guest speakers about competition around the world. The final session consists of a mini-workshop on the latest research on skills and competence, bringing in external faculty and twenty-five additional high-potential women from other Fortune 100 companies to further strengthen participants' networks outside of AT&T.[59] To help the women forge a powerful network, the women are divided at the outset of the program into groups of two or three "learning partners" with whom they build relationships throughout the year, learning about one another's jobs, inviting each other to staff meetings, sharing protégés and mentors, and brainstorming together. Finally, the program gives each participant the opportunity to meet with senior leaders and ask questions that, in any other setting, would not be possible. As a result of this exposure, relationship building, and learning, a number of women have been promoted or placed in more influential positions. Each of these women has, in turn, taken on three new protégés: one from within their department and two from outside. Many have become leadership bloggers on internal sites where they talk about the value of their experiences, helping to change the conversation about leadership and inspire confidence in mid-career women that executive positions will deliver on both their ambitions and most cherished values.

CHANGE THE CONVERSATION

A leader in pharmaceutical sales shared with us an example of how easily the conversation might be changed to alter women's perceptions. Her sales force, she explained, was fifty-fifty men and women at entry- and mid-levels of responsibility, but at the regional director level, the job was overwhelmingly held by men. Committed to diversifying the ranks of her company's leadership, she commissioned an informal study to better understand why women fell off the director track. What she learned was that the men in director roles bragged of putting in sixteen-hour days and weekends spent on the road away from their families. When she polled the men, their description of the job didn't align with what the women had reported: while the work was certainly demanding, their jobs didn't require a 24/7 commitment nor constant overnight travel. "But clearly they enjoyed talking about the heroic measures they took," she told us. "Their talk of sacrifice and hardship was all part of maintaining a macho culture they'd established among themselves—guys one-up each other with this kind of endurance contest conversation. Whereas their female reports were listening to this in all seriousness, saying, 'No way is that job for me.'" So she gathered her regional directors and asked that they make a conscious effort to abide by a different script. She had them talk up the perks and autonomy of their role with female candidates they were looking to promote, and she urged them to encourage explicitly those women whom they most wanted to motivate. The result? Two years after commissioning the study, about a third of those regional director roles were filled by women. "Women need to be told that they have what it takes to run the business, and that they'll get the support they need to succeed in it," she observes. "That joke about women applying for a job only if they meet one-hundred percent of the criteria and men applying for a job if they can spell the title? That rings pretty true in my experience."

INITIATE THE CONVERSATION

Women need to hear from leaders what the next job level entails; they also need to be able to air their concerns.

Talent specialists concur that early coaching, consistent mentoring, and an ongoing, honest dialogue with talent managers give women the input they need to say yes to the stretch opportunities that put them on track for leadership. "Men are all in from the start," observes Valerie Grillo of American Express, "whereas women want the full picture before they make a decision. We get a lot more questions from women on what the job will take, how much travel it entails, whether they have what it takes to succeed. They're willing to do what it takes—provided they feel they actually *know* what it will take."

Jennifer O'Lear, director of corporate HR development and engagement and chief diversity officer for Merck Group, agrees. "Women need a more directed approach to their careers earlier on, so they seek out and grab roles that will give them the overseas experience, sales experience, and profit-and-loss experience they'll need for leadership positions later on," she says. "That's why derailment happens during their thirties and forties: if they haven't got that experience already, it's much more difficult to go out and get it then."

CULTIVATE THE CONVERSATION

Talking to women about power and leadership is a conversation that senior women, and not just HR specialists, should be having with junior women, our senior-level interviewees concur. Women who have broken through to the executive ranks are creating forums where they can informally chat with junior women about the positive aspects of wielding power. At Bank of America, female leaders launched the Global Women's Conference, which brought together more than three hundred senior female leaders from all lines of business and locations throughout the firm, as well as representatives from key markets. The event has led to a continuing agenda of initiatives related to women's empowerment and advancement of goals for the larger issues of diversity and inclusion. A critical component to the success of these programs is visible support and sponsorship from senior female leaders. "Women want to know how other women have handled trying to balance a new baby with a demanding job and how to network effectively across the company," says Cynthia Bowman, chief diversity and inclusion officer at Bank of America. "The informal mentoring that goes on in these circles by women who've powered through is incredibly impactful."

WHAT INDIVIDUALS CAN DO

Indeed, our research points to the necessity of having women who *are* flourishing—who are enjoying the autonomy, agency, and impact that power confers— take every opportunity to communicate to up-and-coming women what a top job will require of them and the many ways in which a top job will reward them. Women who can speak to the joys of success need to do so, whether through company-organized forums or roles in the larger community.

Sandy Lucas, chief operating officer of GE Capital UK, is one leader who is helping change the conversation, in part by modeling the good life, and in part by talking to younger women about how to attain it. Her lifestyle is enviable: She goes out regularly with her friends to restaurants, galleries, and the theater. She works out with a personal trainer, takes long runs in the countryside, and cooks up a storm. Come weekends she will head out of London for a short holiday, or host one of her three nephews. She is flourishing, she says, because her high-demand job allows her to realize her gifts in developing talent and building teams to deliver superlative results. With oversight of operations, IT, sourcing, business transformation, and strategic projects, she is responsible for 170 employees in GE Capital's UK offices.

While that's a lot of impact to have, Lucas strives to extend her influence to women outside of GE. She's coleading GE's women's network across Europe, the Middle East, and Africa, whose fifteen thousand members span thirty-five countries, and sitting on the board of City Women's Network. "I feel it's my responsibility to help these women fulfill their leadership aspirations," she says, "because that's what others did for me: coached me, gave me opportunities, let me make some mistakes, and created an environment for me to develop."

The power of female role models to change the conversation about leadership cannot be overstated. But men, too, have a vital role to play. Like many female leaders we've spoken to, Isabel Gomez Vidal, a managing director who heads up Europe, Middle East, and Africa sales at Moody's Analytics, credits her global leadership role not only to the example set by strong female managers early in her career but also to the sponsorship and support she's gotten from her boss. It was he who proposed she jump from software sales to managing the entire European sales force, a move she hesitated to make because she was pregnant with her second child. He persuaded her to accept the position, which he was vacating, by continually demonstrating how power could be used in positive and impactful ways.

"It's not just that he makes the right decisions and the right judgment calls," she explains. "He puts an agenda forward that people should be treated with respect, and he's pushing this agenda in the organization. It's his level of seniority that lets him do that; otherwise, he couldn't." Inspired by his example, Gomez Vidal not only took on the top EMEA sales job but also became co-executive sponsor of Moody's UK LGBT & Allies employee resource group. Both roles, she says, fulfill her desire to make the world a better place by empowering others. As a champion of diversity, she's been partnering with external organizations, growing her network outside of Moody's to build a platform with an impact beyond what she imagined possible as an individual. "It's a circle: I'm taking my agenda to work, and work is making my agenda possible. The learning I'm doing, the people I'm meeting, the influence I'm exercising—it's great." Indeed, she feels as though her most cherished goal of showing others what they can achieve by growing their confidence in themselves is precisely what her ambassadorship is helping. "There's no question," she says, "that the bigger my voice, the greater my impact."

Gomez Vidal believes that by showing women how leadership can magnify their impact and agency, more women are likely to pursue it, even during those years when pushes and pulls in their personal lives conspire to drag them off course.

"The vast majority of people think it's not possible to have both a high-impact career and a family life, to do it all," Gomez Vidal reflects. "I encourage women to see the bigger picture of what's possible. It's important to show them they can make a difference in the world, one on one, yes, but also as part of the organization." She adds, "And we can help them see that bigger picture. It's important we build their confidence so they exceed what they believe is possible."

4

Arm All Women to Win Sponsorship

In her late thirties, Jessica,* an assistant vice president with a global telecommunications business, very nearly stalled out. She'd advanced quickly, gotten married, and had a child, but she was bored and unfulfilled. "I wanted to enjoy the work I did, and be really good at it," she says, reflecting on that period. "I wanted to be viewed as someone who was the best. But I didn't have a clear objective."

Part of the reason why, she explains, was because she didn't see other women of color ahead of her. As a black woman, she accepted that she'd have to work twice as hard; she just wasn't convinced it would pay off. "Senior people tend to put people who look like them in senior roles," she observes.

But that all changed when a senior African American who saw Jessica's leadership potential talked her up within his circle, introducing her to a leader who steered her into a start-up within the company, where she was put in charge of building its customer service management organization. His advocacy, coupled with her stellar performance, helped Jessica gain visibility at the topmost tiers of the firm: today, she is chief of staff for a team that reports directly to the chairman.

Now she's intent on attaining an executive position, which she sees as likely in five years. "I tell my daughter it's critical to have goals," says Jessica. "But you also need people who can appreciate your brand, and share it with others, so you get the development—and the opportunities—you need to demonstrate your leadership."

THE POWER OF ADVOCACY FROM ABOVE

Research that CTI has been conducting since 2010 shows that a sponsor is critical to career progression.[60] As Stephanie's story demonstrates, a sponsor lends critical career traction by making key introductions, providing stretch assignments, and protecting their rising stars as they grow into those roles.

But because sponsors bestow this powerful backing on individuals whom they trust to burnish their reputation and carry forward their legacy, sponsorship has historically been conferred by white men on other white men—a habit that has culminated in the so-called Boys' Club. Women struggle to attract sponsors for a host of reasons, many of which we've documented in our research: unconscious bias, deeply entrenched leadership norms, a tendency among leaders to make social overtures to people who remind them of themselves, and a well-founded fear of running afoul of sexual harassment policies. These factors conspire to keep the Boys' Club both male and white.

How can we better arm women—particularly those who are confident, and ready, willing, and able to lead—to win sponsorship? By taking a two-pronged approach: leaders need to be incentivized and supported in sponsoring "outside their comfort zone"; women need to be coached on how to make themselves visible, indispensable, and a safe bet. Both companies and individuals, that is, have a role.

WHAT COMPANIES CAN DO

Educating women as to what sponsorship is—how it works and why they need it—is a vital first step.

Women misunderstand the difference between mentorship and sponsorship, we find. Talent specialists tell us that, impelled by their deep need to make a positive difference in others' lives, women on track for top jobs all too readily expend energy mentoring junior women. But mentoring doesn't create opportunities or visibility that results in promotion for the mentee. It's also a one-way expenditure on the part of the mentor, an outreach that may feel good but doesn't earn returns in the form of a deepened talent bench or extended capacity.[61] So high-potential women who over-mentor wind up spread too thin to make a real difference in junior women's careers, and too depleted to cultivate sponsors for themselves.

That sets up a vicious cycle, as sponsors, our research affirms, impact pay (in that they empower their protégés to ask for raises) and promotion (by steering their protégés into stretch assignments and high-visibility projects). Indeed, the "sponsor effect" can be measured in how many more women are satisfied with their career advancement with a sponsor in their corner, as opposed to women who lack that backing (a 19 percent differential, we find).

To ensure that women find sponsors, many companies have set up formal programs wherein high-potential women are matched with senior leaders. Assigning sponsorship can be tricky: the relationship works best when it arises from trust built over time. But because senior men are hesitant to make overtures to junior women that might be misconstrued, and because the social chasm can feel insurmountable between white superiors and black subordinates, such programs can help "prime the pump" for sponsorship to become an aspect of corporate culture. Indeed, talent specialists believe sponsorship will occur between black women and white men only if they structure programs to jump-start interaction.

Companies encourage sponsor relationships in other ways, however, often by planning more one-on-one networking opportunities between high-potential women and leaders who should know about them. American Express, among the first to recognize that sponsorship might be formalized as a career lever, takes a two-pronged approach with programs like *Women in the Pipeline* and *Pathways to Sponsorship,* global initiatives implemented in 2009 that both raise women's consciousness about sponsorship and help connect women to leaders without specifically matching them. Seventy percent of participants in *Pathways* were either promoted or moved into a strategic lateral role, resulting in greater representation of women at the firm's topmost levels and greater engagement of high-potential women overall. "We're seeing big value as a company in *Pathways,*" says Julie Pope, vice president of global talent acquisition for American Express. "Part of it is helping women understand that sponsors can give them visibility, and make them known, in ways they're comfortable with. But part of it too is having leaders say to our high-potential women, 'I'll do what I can to keep you engaged, to help you through a period in your life when you may need more flexibility, because I believe in your long-term leadership potential.'" Additionally, says Pope, "when we give these women flexibility when they need it most, they more than pay back their sponsors: they emerge from their part-time stint with renewed commitment to the firm and their own aspirations. And once they attain, through sponsorship, real power, they then look for ways to empower others. The conversation at women's networks now is, 'Who are you sponsoring?'" Pope explains, "*Pathways* satisfies some of that need to give back to others by allowing women to pay it forward."

Trevor Gandy, chief culture officer at Chubb Group of Insurance Agencies, favors programs that allow rising stars to showcase their leadership skills to potential sponsors, rather than talk about them. A suite of programs at Chubb, for example, gives professionals of color precisely that showcase: they're tasked with solving business challenges that senior managers have identified as imperative, working alongside each other for months at a time. When managers go through development programs alongside high-potential women, Gandy says, they become invested in the women's success—not just in their current role, but in their careers at Chubb.

Would-be sponsors must also be made aware of unconscious bias, talent specialists concur, and be incentivized to address it. They may be scrutinizing a black woman's executive presence against "acceptable" leadership norms; they may also be unaware of the stereotypical assumptions they harbor. To make leaders conscious of "insider/outsider dynamics" and their effect on hiring, promotion, and leadership tracking and development, the Depository Trust & Clearing Corporation (DTCC), an American post-trade financial services company, recently commissioned the Dagoba Group to take the entire executive management team through its inclusive leadership program, which consisted of a four-hour workshop and a follow-up session after six weeks. "Each leader had to create an action plan to minimize the impact of their biases on daily business decisions," says Nadine Augusta, director of diversity and inclusion and corporate social responsibility at DTCC. To ensure that each leader implements his or her plan, Augusta's team will be looking at 360-survey feedback and other survey results measuring inclusivity.

Holding leaders accountable, all agree, is the only way to ensure the Boys' Club comes to include women and minorities. Indeed, at companies where black women quite visibly occupy the top jobs, employees report a virtuous cycle: incoming talent of color feel welcome and included, so they give voice to their ambitions and find support in their bid for leadership roles. Angela Daker of White & Case, for example, says making partner hadn't been part of her vision for herself until "people who didn't look like me encouraged me, based on my work and my potential, to think of the possibilities here." Daker's colleague Denise Diallo, who is one of five black women in White & Case's Paris office, similarly affirms that, as a result of the firm's Women's Initiative and a rich pipeline of black women graduating from elite law schools, White & Case "has made real progress in this regard."

WHAT INDIVIDUALS CAN DO

This is not to suggest, however, that women are obliged to wait for management to recognize and address its own blind spots. On the contrary, our interviewees identify a number of ways in which they've succeeded in overcoming the barriers that deny them sponsorship.

TARGET THE RIGHT PEOPLE

Our own research shows that women tend to target the wrong individuals for sponsorship. They set their sights on role models, or mentors—women they admire, women they like, women they hope to become, but not necessarily women in a position to help them. Specifically, we find, they look to collaborative leaders—those whose style they wish to emulate—even though what's on offer, by and large, are traditionalists who abide by strict hierarchy.[62] Affinity, in other words, guides women in their selection of a sponsor.

Yet, affinity cannot be a primary consideration—because for sponsors to give their protégés career traction, they need one characteristic above all others: a position of power. Sylvia Ann Hewlett learned this lesson the hard way. As a young professor at Barnard, she developed a close relationship with an older colleague, Annette Baxter, whose kindness, integrity, and professionalism aligned with Hewlett's own values. "Annette gave me a great deal," Hewlett recalls of their relationship. "She boosted my confidence and soothed my soul when I felt overwhelmed by the demands of a premature baby on top of the pressures of a high-octane job." But, despite her invaluable support and friendship, Annette turned out to be a poor choice of sponsor: embroiled in a feud with the departmental chair, she had negative political clout at Barnard; as a scholar of medieval history, her influence in Hewlett's discipline of economics was nonexistent. When Hewlett came up for tenure, Annette's backing meant very little to any of the decision makers. Partially as a result of a lack of effective sponsorship, Hewlett's bid for tenure was denied. A month later, she was packing up her office.

Hewlett was devastated. "I had plowed twelve years of my life into my academic career only to have it all tossed aside," she recalls. "I felt bewildered, betrayed, and cast out." But eventually, Hewlett regrouped. "I'd learned my lesson on the sponsorship front," she says now. "I understood that climbing the ladder in any competitive field required heavy-duty support from a powerful, senior person—kindness just wouldn't cut it." Hewlett chose her next sponsor with power at the forefront of her mind. Her new sponsor, Harvey Picker, was dean of the School of International Affairs at Columbia University and former CEO of Picker Instruments. He was a senior leader, with heft and influence in the wider world of economics. He was also a white male.

The fact is, those in power are often neither female nor black nor collaborative in their leadership style. Women need to target white men. Black women, even more than white, need to target white men, because even though white men reflexively sponsor other white men, they are more inclined than minority executives, we find, to extend their advocacy to minority talent. This is true for two reasons: they are far less likely than black executives (5 percent vs. 15 percent) to perceive protégés of color as less qualified than white talent, and they are less likely to be burdened by the perception that they're playing favorites. Black executives are 7.5 times more likely than white to say that sponsoring a person of color will be perceived as favoritism.[63]

Successful women grasp this. They are targeting people with power, and they are not waiting for blinders to lift: they're peeling them off. One director at a Silicon Valley monolith, for example, chose as her potential sponsor one of the senior-most men at the firm. She set up a meeting in which she apprised him of her skills and the value she could bring to his mission, and then laid out what she wanted from him, both to help drive her own career and to enlist him in the firm's agenda of hiring more professionals of color. "You have to be that direct," she explains. "You have to ask for his commitment, and, once he's invested, you have to hold him accountable." She says her sponsor, who is white, has more than stepped up to the plate, and that as a result of his advocacy, she's meeting her goals as well as the firm's. "I'm here to make a difference," she says. "I don't think black women get real power until we get better representation—and that won't happen without the support of those who are in power now."

Celeste,* a partner at a prominent Washington, DC law firm, chose her sponsor, a woman, on the basis of her office décor: red walls, a striped carpet, and a bottle of Maker's Mark on the bookshelf indicated she was an equity partner, since only equity partners had license to customize their environment (and not hide their bourbon!). "I went in and introduced myself," Celeste recalls. "I told her I'd love to work with her in any way. If she needed me to wash her car, or handle a deposition—whatever she needed, I'd be there for her. And when she gave me work, I made double triple sure I did my best." Despite the vast differences in their backgrounds—Celeste had grown up a biracial kid in an Alabama project, whereas her white sponsor came from a middle-class Arizona family—the two women became friends. "We were worlds apart, but by throwing myself in her path, and doing whatever she needed and delivering on it, I got her past that awkwardness," Celeste explains. "It turns out there are tons of things we have in common."

She used a similar approach with the head of her practice group, a white guy. "I delivered really great work, then I made an effort to get to know him," she says. "I found ways to be around him: I'd take the same flight back from a deposition, so we'd be stuck together, and we would have to talk. I asked questions; he talked about himself, about how he and his wife met—and we got past the awkwardness. I'm no longer foreign to him. I am his 'quirky friend,' as opposed to this alien woman he doesn't get."

On track to make equity partner herself, Celeste insists that nothing short of forthrightness would have won her the sponsorship she needed from these senior partners. "You have to put yourself in the way, so that you'll be there when stuff that matters happens. That's a Herculean task for some, I know. But when you are mixed race in Alabama, no one wants you, so you learn to make your own group. That experience as a child taught me to be forward. Now I tell other women, take a shot, loosen up and put yourself out there. It matters so much in so many different ways to get over the 'I know you think we have nothing in common,' and 'Whatever will we talk about?'" She adds, "It's up to us women to get men over that."

MAKE YOURSELF INDISPENSABLE

After her sophomore year of college at Princeton, Mellody Hobson came home to Chicago to work at Ariel Investments as a summer intern. Determined to prove herself, Hobson worked weekends as well as a full work week. "I'd come in, clean off my desk, and look for things to do," she recalls. In particular she wanted to impress the firm's founder, John Rogers. So one Saturday, when the mail bag arrived, Hobson determined she would go ahead and sort it. "John was obsessed with his mail," she explains. She emptied the bag on the floor at the front of the office and got to work creating piles for John and each of his staff. She was sitting among the piles when Rogers came through the door. "What are you doing? Why are you doing it? Who told you to do this?" he asked Hobson. She responded, "I thought it would be nice, since you come in Saturday afternoon, to put aside your mail for you. No one told me to do it."

"I can remember the look on his face," Hobson says. "When he saw me on the floor sorting that bag, a light went on, and he thought, 'Holy s—, she's a keeper!'"

It had been her mother's advice, says Hobson, that she make herself indispensable "She told me, 'You're not going to get fired if they can't live without you,'" recalls Hobson. "And something about that hit home."

Rogers was the first of two key sponsors she won over with her work ethic and loyalty. Bill Bradley, the former US senator, was the other. Hobson volunteered for his campaign while working for Rogers at Ariel. Rogers had some advice for her. "It's about that organization, that person, it's not about you or what you get out of it," he told her. "If you act with only their best interests at heart, it'll pay you in spades in ways you cannot foresee." Rogers was absolutely right, says Hobson, noting that, later in her career, it was Bradley who introduced her to Howard Schultz, CEO of Starbucks, who subsequently invited her to sit on his board. "It was a great lesson, one that I give to others," she concludes. "Believe and trust and have faith in people, and they will do the right thing by you—especially if you act in their interest!"

MAKE YOURSELF A SAFE BET

✓ *Don't "date" (or have an affair with) a supervisor.*
Yes, this is stating the obvious, but it still happens—
and the consequences are almost always more
dire for the woman's career. Our research shows
that conducting an office romance can seriously
undermine your professional credibility on the job.
Worse, the buzz you generate may keep sponsors
external to the firm from throwing you a lifeline.

✓ *Relentlessly telegraph professionalism.* Don't send
mixed messages. If you want to be judged strictly on
your track record, negotiating savvy, management
skills, or market knowledge, don't assert your
sexuality in professional discussions, even if the
other party has brought his or her own sexuality
into the conversation.

✓ *Keep your boss apprised of relationships you're
nurturing off-site.* This is particularly important if
you're young and single, as one young investment
banker learned the hard way. A client whom she
befriended as an occasional tennis partner asked her
for help reviewing documents in preparation for an
initial public offering. She succeeded in persuading
him to let her bank handle his IPO, landing for her
firm the biggest deal of the year. But because it was
a *fait accompli* by the time her boss got wind of it,
he took her off the account, convinced she'd won

it by having an affair with the client. "People will jump to the worst conclusions when they're caught by surprise," she observes. "It's sexist and unfair, but at that stage the damage is already done. Keep people informed from the start, and you'll nip those assumptions in the bud."

✓ *Meet your sponsor "in the public eye."* Frequent one-on-one meetings can work—provided they're not behind a closed office door. Take coffee into the conference room, meet for lunch on campus, or choose a restaurant where you can take the opportunity to wave to people you know and make it clear you have nothing to hide. Dinner on a business trip may be unavoidable, but make sure the venue isn't the kind of place you'd ever go on a date, and don't order alcohol.

✓ *Routinize sponsor meetings.* Regularity is what ensures nothing will appear irregular about meeting a superior of the opposite sex. A standing monthly appointment in a conference room looks more professional than ad hoc or informal meetings.

✓ *Talk about your significant others.* Make known the extent of your outside commitments. Put photos on your desk or choose a screensaver that will assure others you have a network of emotional ties outside of work. You want to assure would-be sponsors that you're a person whose emotional needs are met, a person who isn't looking for anything from a work relationship except professional enrichment.

✓ *Introduce your significant others to your sponsor.* If you are currently in a relationship, take advantage of office social occasions to introduce your spouse or partner. Even if your sponsor is not present, you will establish to everybody else that you're in a stable relationship, making it less likely that tongues will wag when you do take that seat on the shuttle next to the COO.

CRACK THE EP CODE

What may also explain why women struggle to attract sponsors is the narrow band of norms that continue to define leadership. A glance at the cover of *Forbes* or *Fortune* or any industry publication reveals what most of us reflexively think, whether we're conscious of it or not: that leaders are white and male. On one if not both counts, of course, women fail to meet the norm. So on the most basic level they are not seen as "leadership material."

Research that CTI has conducted since 2013 on executive presence reveals that while women and minorities may not look the part, they can help others see them as leaders by acting, speaking, and dressing the part—what we call executive presence, which at most firms is an unwritten but much-cherished set of guidelines for determining who gets tapped for top jobs. Executive presence, or EP, derives from three things: gravitas (do you act like a leader?); communication (do you sound like a leader?); and appearance (do you look like a leader?). All aspiring leaders—white, black, male, and female—must master all three elements of EP to attract powerful backers.[64]

Women who have broken through to leadership do ascribe their success in part to having cracked the EP code at their firm. Some credit early exposure to role models who radiated gravitas; others describe the lessons they learned by paying close attention to superiors who modeled EP. One senior VP at a multinational financial services corporation named Nicole,* for example, says she internalized leadership behaviors from her mother, a PhD who is the head of the Neurology department at a large medical school. "She was always perceived as a woman with answers, a woman who could deliver a tough message, who made leaders out of others," she recalls. But Nicole then had the good fortune, after law school, of working at an aerospace company for "a consummate professional"— an older white male who knew his craft and made sure she shadowed him as a new hire. "So many good habits I got from him, that have stayed with me," she says. "I'm shocked when people miss the mark on these things that play such a significant role in developing followership and credibility. When people don't have it—people who know their craft and are really bright but haven't cracked the code on gravitas—you see micro-inequities plague them. They're marginalized and discounted as a result."

But what gets in the way of acquiring EP, for women and people of color, is the price of conforming: to comply with the leadership code is, by definition, to compromise one's authenticity, because the code was written by white men. Our data calls out this tension: some 72 percent of black women say that EP at their firm means conforming to white male norms (compared to 44 percent of white women), and 34 percent feel they're sacrificing personal authenticity in bowing to these norms (compared to 31 percent of white women). What's interesting is that 30 percent of white men, too, feel they've sacrificed an important aspect of their identity. EP demands we all cover our authentic selves, to a degree.[65]

Successful women have made their peace with this. They describe how, early in their careers, meeting the EP bar demanded that they cover or downplay aspects of themselves, a sacrifice of authenticity that they resented having to make. Keisha Bell, vice president of risk governance, analysis, reporting, and program management at DTCC, recalls questioning whether advancing at her prior company was possible without sacrificing much of her identity. Finance was overwhelmingly white, male, and straight; Bell is black, female, and openly gay. But it was only a fleeting moment of hesitation, she says. "I realized that what I thought was me being 'true' to myself was *also* limiting," she observes. "I realized that unless I owned my own company, I was going to have to fit into *some* kind of norm or construct. So why not this one?" She wasn't going to hide who she was; she simply was going to play by an alternative set of rules, which she'd learned as a child attending a virtually all-white private high school in Brooklyn Heights. "As I matured, it became easier," she says of her executive presence. "I learned that it's okay to adjust to the culture—corporate or otherwise—without sacrificing who you truly are."

Indeed, having used that executive presence to acquire power, Bell says that she is able to be more true to herself and her passions than she ever thought possible. "As I have taken on more senior positions, I find my voice growing louder, both inside this organization and outside," she observes. "I suspect that being female and being black held me back early on—and being lesbian definitely played into my lack of advancement. But now? I get asked to sit on boards, on steering committees, on diversity initiatives, and I provide direction that is absolutely true to who I am."

TALK UP EXTERNAL LEADERSHIP ROLES

Black women are twice as likely as white women to be role models in their communities, a data finding embodied by virtually every black woman we have interviewed. They are serving on boards and spearheading social justice initiatives. They are mentoring young black women; they're also building an extraordinary network of individuals whom they can count on to deepen their bench, extend their reach, and burnish their brand.

Successful women leverage their leadership credentials in both directions. Susan Chapman-Hughes of American Express is a case in point. In addition to running global corporate payments for the US Large Market, she also serves on the boards of the Potbelly Corporation, the National Trust for Historic Preservation in Washington, A Better Chance, The Dean's Advisory Board at the University of Wisconsin-Madison School of Business, and Girls Inc. She mentors young people and looks for every opportunity to support them in her community. This extraordinary level of involvement and commitment speaks to Chapman-Hughes's passions. But it also represents a very conscious strategy to leverage leadership opportunities inside the firm to win powerful roles outside of it; and to use those external roles to push for greater responsibility at American Express.

Chapman-Hughes's 2014 appointment to the board of Potbelly Corporation, the Chicago-based sandwich enterprise, came about because of her visibility at American Express: she was invited to join a minority-held public company in part to help diversify its board. In her mid-forties at the time, she hesitated to accept; she had planned to join a corporate board later in life. But she saw it as the perfect opportunity to propel her growth within American Express—and indeed, the experience has helped steepen her career trajectory. Her current leadership position within global corporate payments (a position she asked for) makes her one of the first operations people ever to get a line role. "I took a big gamble," she says. "I turned down opportunities to quickly go to the next level in operations because I wanted a profit-and-loss role and didn't want to hit a ceiling in my career; I knew I needed to round out my skills. The learning curve was steep, but I've gotten the hang of it."

Indeed, what ensures her effectiveness in her new role is the extraordinary network she has built over the years, not only as a result of her five-year tenure at the firm but also because of her Potbelly board role and other external involvements. "I've worked hard to earn influence," she says. "I've been able to build strong, broad sponsorship across the organization. If I need to get something done, there are a lot of people who are willing to help me. Being successful here depends on that. That's my brand. I stand up for my people, for my clients, and that resonates: it buys me the opportunity to have even greater power and influence."

Chapman-Hughes sees her role at American Express as a way to amplify her impact on the greater community, too. "I look at this current opportunity as a gift," she reflects. "I'm in a position to leverage power to change what I'm most passionate about. I couldn't do what I do, to help those in my community, to help young people, to help the boards I serve on, if didn't have the American Express brand to support that work."

LEAD WITH A YES

Joanna Coles, editor in chief at *Cosmopolitan*, describes how she won her first television role, presenting news on BBC2, the UK network: the show's intended moderator had a heart attack en route to the BBC studios and died.

"They called me at four thirty that afternoon and said, can you come in and do the show at nine thirty tonight?" she says. "It was one of those things. I wasn't ready; I didn't know anything about the subject matter. But I absolutely knew that I had to seize the opportunity."

So she did, even though it meant canceling a dinner party. "I said, 'Of course I can be there, how soon do you need me? What do you need me to do?'" she recalls. She made a good enough job of it, moreover, to be invited back. "I presented a rather ramshackle, flung together show but it was live television and that is what you do. It was an incredibly good experience. I presented more shows, and then we moved to the US."

Yet women she manages today seem not to recognize an opportunity when they are handed it, she observes. While at *Marie Claire*, Coles recalls, she ran into Jennifer Westfeldt, who was directing her movie, *Friends with Kids,* on the Upper West Side. "I said to her, 'We ought to do something to publicize this.' She said, 'Why don't you send someone?'" So Coles turned to a junior person whose work had impressed her and asked if she would go interview Westfeldt. "She said, 'Sorry, I've got a Super Bowl party that afternoon,'" says Coles, laughing with incredulity. "I just couldn't believe that she would rather hang out with her friends than go and interview a female director on the set of her movie for a piece in the magazine," she continues. "It was her job, really, to go and do it." She adds, "It told me a lot about her."

Sponsors are looking for protégés who lead with a yes. We know from our 2012 survey that sponsors say that attitude is hugely important. Fifty-seven percent agreed that a "can-do attitude" was critical in would-be protégés; 44 percent agreed that subordinates must deliver a 110-percent effort to earn their sponsorship. Among would-be protégés, however, only 32 percent recognize the importance of leading with a yes. "There are times in life when you just have to show up," counsels Coles. "It may not be convenient, but I assure you, for your career prospects it is absolutely critical."

MAKE DIFFERENCE YOUR DISTINCTIVE CURRENCY

Data from our 2012 report on sponsorship affirms that "bringing a different set of skills and/or perspective" is a priority for protégés (according to 38 percent of respondents), along with innovating solutions (39 percent) and offering big-picture thinking (39 percent).[66] That has implications for all women in search of sponsors, of course. But for black women, what may not be obvious is that race is a differentiator to be embraced when it comes to cultivating sponsors with a distinctive set of skills, insight, or innovation.

Successful black women we interviewed explained in detail how they leveraged insights gained from growing up in or working in communities that were utterly foreign to their white colleagues. A black woman who had spent twenty years in Seattle's black neighborhoods as a loan officer for Washington Mutual, for example, succeeded in helping American Express grow market share among small- to medium-enterprise minority business owners by sharing her knowledge of this underserved target market, crafting—and patenting!—a segmented marketing strategy.

The innovation needn't drive revenues to attract attention. Back when Monica Poindexter, head of diversity and inclusion for Roche Diagnostics, worked as a recruiter at Genentech, she noticed that every one of the firms competing with hers for diverse talent had a scholarship for students of color who were pursuing degrees in science. Working with the firm's leadership funding and corporate relationship groups, Poindexter put together a strategy; working with professors, she identified programs and determined allocations. Within a year, under her leadership, the program launched. By the time it ended (in 2009, when the firm was acquired by Roche, a medical technology developer), it had given out $875 thousand in scholarships and brought thirty to forty graduates of color into Genentech's workforce.

Performance and loyalty are the pillars on which sponsorship rests. But they are not sufficient. To attract sponsors and stand out among other stellar performers, women must identify and develop a brand or currency that sets them apart, as Poindexter did—a unique perspective, an innovative approach, or a network of relationships that no one else has. And then they must have the courage to assert it. "That's how I built my brand," says Poindexter. "I closed that gap, and people took notice."

PART THREE:
WHAT SUCCESS LOOKS LIKE

A ll women want five things: the ability to flourish, to excel, to reach for meaning and purpose, to be empowered and empower others, and to earn well. Ambition manifests in myriad and marvelous ways, however: success is as individually defined as the women who have achieved it. In this section, we showcase women who have harnessed power in ways both inspiring and instructive.

5

Flourishing

In the 1980s, as a new member of the esteemed Council on Foreign Relations, Sylvia Ann Hewlett recalls being taken aside by CFR's only female board director for a bit of sisterly advice. The board member, an officer of the General Motors Corporation and its chief economist, congratulated Hewlett on being one of only three women to be elected to CFR that year. She was an admirer of Hewlett's scholarly work on emerging markets and had championed Hewlett's candidacy, but she had a word of warning. "I see some of your recent work centers on the male-female wage gap," this board member counseled her. "As a woman economist, you must take care not to dilute your reputation by getting involved in these soft women's issues. They will contaminate you." Patting Hewlett on the arm, she added, "Better to focus on growth models."

Hewlett recoiled. Though she knew this female leader meant well, nothing about women's issues struck her as soft. While teaching at Barnard early in her career, Hewlett had taken a short break to deal with a difficult pregnancy and a dangerously premature child;

when she returned to work a mere eight months later, she found that she hadn't won tenure and was out of a job. As Hewlett saw it, women in the US were worse off than women elsewhere in the advanced industrial world. In countries such as France, Italy, Sweden, and even the UK, working mothers had access to a rich array of maternity and childcare benefits; as a result, the wage gap in these countries was much narrower than in the US. Ignoring the board member's advice, Hewlett penned *A Lesser Life: The Myth of Women's Liberation in America*, an indictment of feminists for failing to improve women's economic lot—the first salvo in a series of analyses that quantified the costs borne by women, but also by society, when working parents are denied material support.

For Hewlett, the fight for women's rights was acutely personal. Born in a small Welsh coal-mining town, Hewlett was the second of six daughters to working-class parents who openly expressed their disappointment that none of their children were sons. With the local coal-mining industry in sharp decline, opportunities for men were already limited; opportunities for women were all but nonexistent. Even as a child, Hewlett understood the second-class status accorded to women, whose lives were confined in the home and dominated by domestic chores. Her own mother reared six kids in a house with no heating other than a coal fire, no refrigerator, no washing machine, and no help. One of Hewlett's vivid memories is of her mother bathing her youngest sister in a tin bath in front of the fire, a bath her mum filled one teakettle at a time. She also remembers helping her mother scrub bed sheets on a board, feed them through the wringer, and hang them outside on a line. In the raw, rain-soaked Welsh winters, bed sheets rarely dried. Days after washing, Hewlett and her sister would be sent to collect them, frozen stiff, from the line. "The relentless toil of women's lives!" Hewlett exclaims. "I was determined to escape it."

If the publication of *A Lesser Life* established Hewlett as a feminist focused on economic conditions, the publication of *When the Bough Breaks: The Cost of Neglecting Our Children*, established Hewlett as an economist focused on child welfare and on policy. This book, which won her a Robert F. Kennedy book award, argued that paid parental leave and subsidized childcare were policy imperatives, not progressive luxuries. Hewlett's research brought her to testify before Congress in 1992, when it was deliberating over the bill that would become the Family and Medical Leave Act—the first legislative triumph of the Clinton Administration.

In the mid-1990s, Hewlett joined forces with Cornel West to write their influential work, *The War Against Parents*, which examined how government policies were throwing up barriers that prevented low-income Americans from nurturing and supporting their children. In 1998, these efforts culminated in Hewlett and West's launch of the "Parents' Bill of

Rights" at a dinner at the White House. Based as it was on the shared struggle of low income Americans (women and men, black and white), this manifesto had considerable impact, seeding a series of town halls in sixty communities across the country. These community conversations spurred new legislation, particularly at the State level. But Hewlett's ability to impact policy faded fast after the election of George W. Bush in 2000. Realizing that, for several years at least, progressive solutions for women, children, and working families would simply not be triggered in Washington, Hewlett turned her attention to the private sector. In 2003, rallying support from her circle of scholars, policymakers, activists, and business leaders, she embarked on a new venture: to bring about employer-led solutions for working women and minorities. In 2003, the Center for Work-Life Policy, Hewlett's own think tank, was born.

Now in its thirteenth year, the Center for Talent Innovation—rebranded in 2012 to reflect the increasing scope of its research—is committed to full realization of the new streams of labor in the global marketplace; to women, yes, but also to people of color and LGBT employees. Today, CTI research is supported by some eighty-seven multinational corporations ranging from GE to Goldman Sachs to Google. These companies employ over six million people in 192 countries around the world. One thing Hewlett is most proud of is the more than three hundred new best practices that have been seeded by CTI studies. She points to the ways in which Center research has driven concrete change: making sponsorship more accessible to women and minorities, fine-tuning flexible work arrangements, establishing off ramps and on ramps, and creating system-wide tools to disrupt bias.

Reflecting back on the progress of recent years, Hewlett feels strongly that neither the private nor the public sectors fully comprehend how societal women's issues are: to deny women support, she believes, is to deny society of the enormous value they have to contribute—both to the bottom line and to making the world a better place. "Women are different from men," she explains. "They want a bigger basket of goods in terms of life goals. So creating a framework that allows women to gain traction is the responsibility of both government and corporations." But it's not about hand-outs, she clarifies. "What's needed is a framework with a wider focus, one that acknowledges that the majority of women are now in the workforce for forty or more years. Policy makers and business leaders need to be a lot more creative in putting front and center women's differentiated needs over the entire lifespan."

Looking back on her own life, Hewlett credits her hardscrabble upbringing for making her clear-eyed about power. Witnessing unemployment and poverty in the coal-mining community of her childhood fueled Hewlett's fierce desire to find better opportunities for herself. And seeing her mother sacrifice everything for her children spurred her to take advantage of changing attitudes towards women to carve out a successful career and raise a family.

"Betty Friedan's pathbreaking book *The Feminine Mystique* meant little to me," Hewlett recalls. "I had no experience of female ennui in white middle class suburbs." Ambivalence towards power, Hewlett notes, was a luxury that she—like many poor women— could not afford; and for that insight she is profoundly thankful. When she came to the US as a graduate student, she could not identify with many of her peers—white women from affluent backgrounds. "I thank my mother every day for showing me that what truly liberates women is independence and economic clout. Without those things, it's hard to have influence or impact." Hewlett acknowledges that the economic barriers she faced differ in scale and scope from the racial barriers that hold back black women. "But in terms of ambition and an understanding of what power can do," she says, "I feel a visceral connection to black women."

GOOD STRESS

Like Hewlett, women who have punched through the glass ceiling consistently speak to the exhilaration and agency they feel in their high-powered roles. They are flourishing, not because they manage to avoid stress, but rather because the demands made upon them tap their powers to the fullest. They welcome situations that require strategic vision and thrill to the task of implementing that vision successfully. They don't shirk the big decisions, either. They derive tremendous satisfaction from setting a new course and steering the corporate ship. Limited resources, demanding stakeholders, and stressful work conditions don't daunt them. On the contrary, such challenges inspire them to raise their game.

Flourishing, as one interviewee put it, is like surfing a monster wave: the exhilaration comes from controlling an intrinsically stressful situation so that it is serving you, instead of you serving it. Maintaining this control demands you marshal your courage and apply every skill you've got. Where others might be crushed, you are able to harness the energy of the situation to reach your goal. "There's nothing quite so thrilling nor rewarding as that," she says. We'd certainly agree.

Decades of research make sense of this seeming contradiction. Stress can be good or bad, depending on the level of control you feel. Back in 1979, Robert Karasek speculated that "decision latitude," or the power to make decisions about how to get work done, might mitigate the negative health effects associated with high-demand jobs.[67] Since then, studies conducted on nurses, accountants, office workers, manufacturing employees, and other types of workers have shown that having decision-making control over where, when, and how work gets done utterly changes the way we respond, physiologically, to stress.[68] Specifically, where workers experience both high levels of demand *and* control, researchers find that challenging situations spur the release of adrenaline but suppress the release of cortisol, the hormone associated with deleterious health effects.[69] In fact, there's ample literature to suggest that we can thrive on stress, and benefit from the hormones it triggers, provided we build into our daily lives physical activity and social support.[70]

Or as one global executive puts it, "bad stress is being at everybody's beck and call," whereas good stress is being in a position to prioritize the demands made upon you, and to delegate to others whatever you can. "I'm creating the agenda, not reacting to it," she explains. "Others prioritize their time to align with mine. Eighty percent of my work is to my timeline." She muses on this and then adds, "I couldn't do a global job, let alone enjoy doing it, without that kind of control."

6

Excelling

Freezing rain. Gale-force winds. Total isolation from family and close-quartered living with eighty coworkers.

And that's a *good* two-week rotation on an oil-drilling platform 110 miles off the coast of Scotland.

For an Offshore Installation Manager (OIM)—the person responsible for anywhere from 80 to 120 platform workers' lives—it can get a lot worse. Jonelle Salter, who at the age of twenty-eight served as an OIM for BP, recalls the intense physical challenge of working an oil rig: at one point, trying to make her way across a North Sea platform to board a chopper, she needed a 220-pound worker to hold onto her life jacket as she crossed over to the helideck to keep her from being blown off the platform. "If it isn't the weather threatening you," she says, "it's the work itself"— pipes bursting, gasses leaking, heavy machinery running amok. On a platform off the coast of Trinidad, Salter recalls, a swinging bucket holding twelve hundred pounds of mud slammed into a worker, nearly killing him.

Even as a new mother, Salter dealt with all of it. On top of the physical and psychological challenges, however, she also had to establish her authority as a young black woman in a sea of middle-aged white men. When she worked off the coast of her native Trinidad, she had a young crew—"very Latin in their attitudes"— that taunted her and tested her leadership, on one occasion holding a meeting without her, even though she was the head of the group, because she was five minutes late. She found her sea-legs; since OIMs are held personally liable for accidents, she couldn't afford to be found wanting in any situation where saving lives required split-second decisions and the unquestioning execution of her orders.

So why, given the all-round duress of the job, and the enormous liability implicit in her role, did she fight for the opportunity to train for it and do it?

"It's awe inspiring to be in charge of the machinery and equipment of an oil platform, not to mention the health and safety of all those men," Salter says. "You train and train, but you still don't know whether you'll be up to the job when an emergency happens. Think of subzero temperatures, everything slick with ice, gale force winds—and then a wall of fire, breaking pipes, oil gushing…"

She reflects a moment, and then adds, "Whether you can conjure up the right kind of leadership, and not get rattled and make mistakes of judgment in these situations is kind of this big test. So that when you pass?" She smiles at the recollection. "You feel quite wonderful."

THE FLYWHEELS OF AMBITION

To those familiar with psychologist Anna Fels's work, women's desire to be challenged, stretched, and not found wanting will come as no surprise. In her 2004 book *Necessary Dreams: Ambition in Women's Changing Lives,* Fels documented women's immense drive to take on difficult things and do them well—what motivation expert Robert White has termed "effectance."[71] But Fels also discerned that, while doing a thing well is rewarding in and of itself, "the pursuit of mastery over an extended period of time requires a specific context: an evaluating, encouraging audience must be present for skills to develop." Mastery cannot be disentangled, she observed, from recognition; affirmation and approval are the motivational engines that drive women to develop expertise. "Without earned affirmation, long-term learning and performance are rarely achieved," she observes.[72]

To excel, then, women need two things: intellectual growth on the job (which 79 percent say is very important) and recognition of their growth and achievement by superiors and peers (as 42 percent find to be critical).

The intellectual growth piece, for women, is absolutely huge. In all our interviews we encountered women rapacious for challenge because they're intent on personal growth, women who choose for themselves daunting jobs precisely because triumphing at them is indisputable evidence that they have excelled. Many of our interviewees define success as personal excellence, and articulate ambition in terms of personal growth. They're clear, too, on which aspects of growth they consider important: 76 percent identify learning new professional skills; a majority also identify becoming more creative and innovative.

Sarah* is one of them. She wants a challenge—the bigger the better. As a VP in consumer insights for a telecommunications provider, she's responsible for consumer retention; as the marketplace grows ever more saturated, it's her job to come up with the data and insights necessary to capture and keep diverse customers. Finding ways for her team to implement their understanding and stay ahead of the competition keeps her on the road and working long hours, a commitment that's necessitated that her husband take the lead role at home raising their seven- and ten-year-old daughters. But Sarah is confident it's the right decision, because she loves making progress in areas where no one else has. "I gravitate to the big problems because solving them gives me a tremendous sense of accomplishment," she explains. "I feel I'm truly making a difference for the company."

Women want challenge badly enough to turn down job offers or resist promotions that threaten to deny them that growth. Consider Desiree Ralls-Morrison,

SVP and general counsel for Boehringer Ingelheim, USA, a top pharmaceutical company. Prior to joining the family-owned pharmaceutical company, Ralls-Morrison worked for Johnson & Johnson, where she spent years exercising her legal and business acumen and moving up the ranks until she found herself promoted out of doing the work she loved. "It was a position with more money, and more influence," she observes. "But I wasn't happy. I wasn't challenged and I wasn't growing." She adds, "Some might see my coming to a smaller company as a lateral move, but I have a lot of autonomy, broad and deep responsibility, and, most importantly, I feel my expertise is being used."

OF FOREIGN LANDS AND PEOPLE

There is another aspect of intellectual growth that women want: 48 percent say that an important aspect of intellectual growth for them in their work is to acquire knowledge of different people and cultures. And while a stunning 34 percent of women in our cohort over the age of forty do not have children, when we compared women with children to women without children, we found no statistical difference in the importance they ascribe to learning about other people and cultures.

Julie Marcello, an industry segment leader in the Financial Institutions Practice for Chubb, does not see her appetite for foreign exposure changing anytime soon.

"I love engaging with people in different cultures," the thirty-eight-year-old American says. "And to engage—to understand what they're facing, to be really clear in your messaging—you've got to travel."

While currently based in New York, in her previous role as Eurozone manager Marcello was on a monthly basis en route from her home in London to Paris, Amsterdam, and other offices on the continent—all part of engaging the 150 people who worked in the management liability insurance specialty business she was overseeing. While she says it can be hard, bridging cultural and language differences, Marcello thrives on meeting the challenge. At fifteen, she lived abroad for a year; at twenty-five, she left the US for South America; at twenty-eight, she moved to Australia; and at thirty-three, she relocated to the UK. "What I find rewarding, personally, is the experience of going for it—of taking the leap into the unknown," she explains. "Early on, it can be rough; resilience is hugely important. But I tell myself this is temporary; I'll find my feet. If it doesn't work out, I tell myself, I can always change it." She adds, "I may find that, with a child, I scale back, but I can't really see staying put for long. It's risk-taking, professionally, that leads to personal growth. Which I find too hugely rewarding to give up anytime soon."

Interviews with women who, like Marcello, have lived in multiple geographies and who, as primary breadwinners, have relocated their families to gain leadership or operational experience, impel us to rethink our assumptions. Much more so than men, women want work to expand their horizons and deepen their knowledge of others—and our qualitative evidence suggests they embrace the risk-taking and elasticity that such growth entails.

7

Reaching for Meaning and Purpose

Risa Lavizzo-Mourey, president and CEO of the Robert Wood Johnson Foundation, the United States' largest philanthropy focused solely on health, readily recalls the point in her career when she realized that, to have lasting and meaningful impact, she would need to come by real power. It was during her residency at Brigham and Women's Hospital in Boston, where she found herself caring for—repeatedly—a woman whom she dubbed Patient Ruth. Mentally ill, unemployed, and living on the streets, Ruth would be admitted to the ER with horrific leg ulcers. Lavizzo-Mourey would clean her up, administer antibiotics, give her a meal, and discharge her the next day. A few weeks later, Ruth would return to the ER, and they'd repeat the drill. The experience reminded Lavizzo-Mourey of her parents, black physicians devoted to improving both the health of their underserved Seattle community and patients' access to healthcare. "It was just clear to me that this was a failing of all of the systems that might keep her healthy," says Lavizzo-Mourey.

And so began her journey to the top of her field, an ever steepening trajectory that began with her stint as chief of geriatric medicine at the University of Pennsylvania's School of Medicine and culminated with her leadership of RWJF, where she drives social transformation of the nation's healthcare system. With the financial muscle of the foundation and her own heightened visibility (she's been on *Forbes*' 100 Most Powerful Women list since 2014), her intent, she says, is to replace the flawed health system that led Ruth back to the ER time and time again with nothing short of a holistic "culture of health" designed to lift the wellbeing of entire communities. [73]

"When you're working on something and you feel there's something more that you could do to make it better, you have to make sure to lean into that," Lavizzo-Mourey says. "I think that was what motivated me, continually. I would see these things that could be addressed—I'm not going to say fixed, because it's not that simple—that had a real impact on people's lives, starting with the individuals I was seeing in front of me, but then gradually on more and more individuals. The fact that I was often the only African American woman in the room, if not one of the only women in the room—I realized I had a perspective that was important to contribute, and an opportunity that was important to keep pursuing, because there weren't any others there pushing in that direction. It was important to bring my experience to the table."

Women tell us they are highly motivated to work when work makes a difference in the world. Fully 78 percent want from work a sense that what they're doing has considerable meaning and purpose. What assures them of that purpose? Seeing their work have a lasting impact on others, both in their profession and outside of it—a breadth of impact that relies upon a certain measure of power and influence.

Women who, like Lavizzo-Mourey, hold jobs in science, engineering, and math-intensive fields may be the most impassioned of all. Some 63 percent of female scientists working in the private sector, we find, say they've chosen to do what they're doing because of a desire to contribute to society's health and wellbeing (as compared to 51 percent of their male colleagues). More women cited altruism as a prime motivator than cited high compensation; five times as many women in science, engineering, and technology (SET) cite altruism as motivating as do those who cite having a powerful position.[74] Women in SET are also significantly more likely than men in the field (51 percent vs. 40 percent) to cite the ability to contribute to the wellbeing of society as a prime motivator in their work/career.[75]

In all functions across all industry sectors, however, women we've interviewed in the last decade describe their yen for impact, for reach that exceeds the immediate confines of the job to make a positive difference in the larger community—something we don't typically hear from men. Denise Strauss is one of these women: she goes to work every day not just to boost her firm's bottom line, but also to advance a social good. As VP of cardiovascular marketing at Boehringer Ingelheim in the US, she manages eighteen individuals who develop material, messaging, and programs for healthcare payers and providers. Her team will make sure, for example, that customers have the tools they need to both help patients transition from a hospital to a nursing home or rehab facility and provide those patients with the consistency of care necessary to improve treatment compliance and reduce hospital readmissions. "I had a vision, out of college, of wanting to make a difference by improving patient health," she says, "and at this firm, I see myself delivering on that." She adds, "It's important to me to be a role model to my family, my peers, and others who aspire to do good and contribute to society."

And black women, even more so than white (85 percent vs. 76 percent), say it's important to be able to reach for meaning and purpose—to have work that allows them to make a positive difference in other people's lives.

MAKING A DIFFERENCE

Coming out of college, Pia Wilson-Body applied to management training programs, not jobs. "I wanted to be in a position to direct other people, to lead," she says.

What shaped that ambition was, to a large extent, her experience at Spelman, a historically black women's college in Atlanta where she did a work study in the office of Christine King Farris, the sister of Dr. Martin Luther King Jr.; where Jesse Jackson announced his run for the presidency while she sat in Sisters Chapel; and where she heard the likes of Alice Walker, Shirley Chisholm, Marian Wright Edelman, Andrew Young, and Maynard Jackson speak. "We got to watch leaders in action," she recalls. She very nearly missed out on those experiences, she says, having set her heart on attending Howard until a last-minute invitation came from Spelman to visit the campus. "I saw the Spelman women walk across campus in their shirts and skirts and jackets with so much pride, and I said to myself, 'I have got to be here,'" she explains. "What appealed to me was their moxie, that take-charge independence that telegraphed, 'You can do it.'"

So when she began her career at a financial services firm as a management trainee, she was very clear on what she wanted leadership to give her: the opportunity to empower others; a path rich with meaning and purpose; and the ability to earn well.

Today, as director of external relations at Intel, Wilson-Body affirms that leadership has indeed delivered on all of that. She has done better, financially, than she ever could have imagined, enabling her and her husband to send their two boys to the best schools, expand their travel horizons, and gain exposure to growth opportunities. And professionally, she is empowered, even mandated to give back: in her current role, she makes key decisions for the company "in terms of where we engage, how we engage, and the partnership opportunities that present themselves." The most meaningful aspect of her job, however, is that she is in a position to connect others with their passions. Designated within the firm as a master mentor, Wilson-Body "puts others on their path," a play to her strengths and fulfillment of her purpose. "When I go into the cafeteria, people come up to me and say, 'Pia, you really helped me,'" she relates. "I didn't help them to get their praise, but to see them grow into their potential. That's what makes this job nirvana."

Women seem particularly impelled to wrest from their careers evidence that they've created options for people who don't have very many, and secured for others the very opportunities that have transformed their own lives for the better. Women are passionate to advance, through work, a portfolio of causes—particularly educational access, women's rights, and health for all.

Nancy Di Dia, who heads up diversity, inclusion and engagement in the US at Boehringer Ingelheim, is a good example. As a passionate advocate of women's rights, patient's rights, and gay rights, she "couldn't be happier" in her job, she says, because her role, and her access to the firm's senior most management, has positioned her to advance each of these important initiatives. In the course of her career she's advocated for adoption of nondiscrimination policies for LGBT employees worldwide and even in states where that protection didn't exist; in leading the cross-functional team to introduce greater diversity into clinical trials, she's ensured better health outcomes for women and minority patient groups; and by helping cancer patients navigate the healthcare system, she's ensuring that those in dire need get the benefits owed to them. "For global diversity, women, and LGBT rights, I'm positioned pretty well to be able to give back," she reflects. "I can impact organizational change, and coach people who are struggling. I feel like I have everything I need to contribute to equality."

Women also say it's important that they work for an organization whose values align with their own. "When I sense that my goals at work no longer track with my personal mission," observes one healthcare consultant and cancer survivor, "then I know it's time to move on. Life's too short to waste my time and energy on moving an agenda I can't really get behind."

MODELING SUCCESS

We find that women judge work to be meaningful when it gives them an opportunity to model success and exceed expectations—their own, and those of their family or community. Fully 73 percent say "achieving goals set before me" is an important aspect of meaning and purpose.

Not surprisingly, those most eager for work to give them the opportunity to prove themselves are those whose own advancement has come at extraordinary cost.

Celeste, the attorney from the prominent Washington, DC law firm, is one of them. As an undergraduate, she saw herself going to law school to pursue a career in public service—a vision she shared with her history professor, whose guidance she cherished. Her professor's response took her by surprise. "Don't be afraid to take a high-powered, high-paid job," she counseled. "Women feel called to jobs that don't pay nearly as much as men's, because it allows them to serve, but there are other ways to serve. You're a leader, Celeste. Look at those executive positions, because we need more women like you to be in them."

Having grown up in an Alabama housing project as a child of mixed race, Celeste wasn't about to abandon her idea of public service. She applied to Vanderbilt Law School intent on gaining the knowledge necessary to help those in her family and community who had suffered at the hands of the system either because they didn't understand or couldn't articulate their rights. While in school, she worked in a district attorney's office.

But she came to see that her professor was right: assuming a powerful position at a law firm was indeed another way to serve.

Today, as a partner in her firm, Celeste feels she has realized her ambition—and then some. Senior enough to be making decisions about recruiting, hiring, and compensation practices, she's able to make a difference for black women who, like her, may not have grown up imagining themselves as high-powered, well-paid lawyers. "If I weren't here," she says, speaking of her seat alongside the chair of the firm's diversity and inclusion committee, "there wouldn't be any black women on that committee, and black women's concerns wouldn't be heard. What motivates me now, in this role, is to bring others along." She adds, "I love being able to do that, and proving that it can be done."

8

Empowered, and Empowering Others

From an early age, Tiffany Eubanks-Saunders, a senior vice president at Bank of America, understood that, provided she worked hard and excelled at school, she would have choices her parents did not. But only when INROADS, the internship program for academically gifted minority students, arranged for her to work at Bank of America the summer after she graduated high school, did Eubanks-Saunders grasp what some of those choices might be. "INROADS exposed me to industries and careers that were not traditional for black people," Eubanks-Saunders recalls. "Among the people I knew, no one aspired to be a banker. You might have aspired to become a doctor, a lawyer, maybe even an accountant, based on images in the media. But banking or financial services just weren't part of the dialogue in a black household."

More importantly, the INROADS experience showed her the kind of person she wanted to become: a leader like Linda Lockman-Brooks. More than twenty years ago, Lockman-Brooks was one of very few black female executives at the bank. She made it her mission to mentor and coach young women like Eubanks-Saunders, creating jobs and carving out opportunities for minority women that wouldn't have existed without her fearless insistence. "Having the opportunity to work for Linda and observe the way she carried herself—the executive presence she modeled, her ability to influence, and her commitment to help others like herself—marked my desire to aspire to a position similar to hers," says Eubanks-Saunders.

So when she graduated *summa cum laude* with an economics degree from North Carolina Agricultural and Technical State University, with job offers from several banks, Eubanks-Saunders chose Bank of America—determined to continue Lockman-Brooks's legacy. "The reason I strive to be at this leadership level or beyond is because it allows me to provide opportunities to the many highly talented females, specifically minority females, who in many instances would not be considered otherwise," says Eubanks-Saunders. "Within the organizations that I lead, nine times out of ten, I am going to have a higher percentage of women and blacks and Hispanics than my peers because I am the only black female at my level for my division. If I don't demonstrate to my peers that you can absolutely find competent diverse talent that meets your business needs and that contributes greater diversity of thought, yielding a richer set of solutions, then no one will. If I don't help to influence change that addresses unconscious bias and counters traditional stereotypes, it simply won't happen."

THE POWER OF CONNECTION

Women want rewarding relationships both in and outside of work. They consider important the ability to empower others, and be empowered, as 68 percent affirm. They want to support others, and be supported; inspire others, and be inspired; learn from others' expertise, and share their own.

At work, they find certain aspects of relationships important: to help them advance in their career (as 50 percent affirm); to provide role models (51 percent); and to connect them to powerful people (24 percent). What a robust majority of women (68 percent) understand to be critical to their careers are aspects of *having* a sponsor. But a majority of women—52 percent—also consider aspects of *being* a sponsor to others important in their career. Women are nearly as eager to empower others as they are to be themselves empowered.

Isabel Gomez Vidal of Moody's Analytics embodies this set of motivations. She hungers to have agency, influence, and impact on the business, but even more so, on other people. With responsibility for more than a hundred people in sales roles across all lines of Moody's Analytics business in Europe, the Middle East, and Africa, Gomez Vidal makes decisions that influence the direction of the company, a role that she never imagined possible for herself when she started eight years ago at Moody's as a sales representative. Yet it's precisely her journey that impels her to want from her career the opportunity to show others, through her leadership, what they are capable of. "I enjoy facing challenges and proving to myself I'm able to do what I never thought I could," Gomez Vidal reflects. "I am enjoying the journey of growing myself to this level and I enjoy having the compensation to support the lifestyle I want. But it's the impact I have on other people's growth that I love the most. I'm a strong believer in building people's confidence so they can achieve what they think is impossible."

Indeed, we find that about one in four women identify being responsible for others' career development as a critical aspect of power. Women recognize the importance of *being* a sponsor to the same degree they recognize the importance of *having* a sponsor.

THE POWER TO MAKE A DIFFERENCE

Black women, even more than white, relish having power as the means by which they can lift up others. They enjoy power because they can empower other black women.

Glenda McNeal, executive vice president of Global Client Group and Strategic Partnerships at American Express, is a good example. Managing the firm's largest merchant relationships demands she be conversant about a multitude of products, services, and operating environments across dozens of companies in all industry sectors in all geographies. In a given week, McNeal explains, she might travel to Asia, build a relationship with a local merchant working through a translator, return to the US to work with Walmart's finance team, and sit down with the chief marketing officer of Hilton. She then takes what she's learned from these client interactions and reports back to the executive team, offering her opinion that in turn will help shape their strategy. "My senior team relies on me to give a point of view, to be thoughtful and credible; because they're going to make decisions on behalf of the company influenced by what I have to say," she explains. It means a lot to her that she's in a position to influence top leaders—something black women far more than white identify as an important aspect of power (32 percent vs. 21 percent).

But it is the example she sets for other women and people of color, McNeal stresses, that makes her powerful role so gratifying. Growing up the last of eight children (and the seventh girl) on a Louisiana farm, McNeal had no role models; no women of color to demonstrate what was possible in the business world, aside from one sister who became a successful accountant. "I've come a long way from a Louisiana farm," she observes. "I had a strong desire to be successful in my career, and I have been. I want the women behind me to see that it's possible. I want my leadership and behaviors to inform others as they manage their careers."

Being responsible for others' career development is something black women are more likely than white

(33 percent vs. 25 percent) to identify as an important aspect of power. Over and over, our interviewees made clear how vital it was to them to be a role model, mentor, or sponsor. Joyce Trimuel, former vice president and Kansas City branch manager at Chubb, describes her role on Chubb's Multicultural Development Council overseeing Project Ignite, a leadership development program, as "the defining moment" of her career, largely because for its eighteen participants (all men and women of color), the initiative proved to be the defining moment of *their* careers. "For people of color coming up through the ranks, who are wondering, 'What will my career trajectory look like?' we can point to people being developed, being considered for opportunities," says Trimuel. "They see me, a woman of color as branch manager, and it gives them hope. They can see there is room for them at the table of a white-male-dominated organization."

Angela Daker of White & Case knew she wanted to be a lawyer as early as high school because, growing up in Chicago's public schools, she saw lawyers as advocates for people who couldn't advocate for themselves. Juvenile justice is a passion of hers, one that impelled her to run a legal clinic right out of law school (on whose board she now sits). Committed to public interest work, for some years she taught criminal justice at Northwestern University. So when she came to White & Case, it wasn't with any intent to make partner: she sought opportunities to mentor and coach associates. As a partner, however, she feels that her impact as a mentor and sponsor is amplified. She's involved in committees, heads up the women's initiative in the Miami office, mentors associates in the firm's black affinity group, and recruits, develops, and advocates for diverse associates and for women. "As I get more senior, I'm able to sponsor others as I've been sponsored," she says.

Tiffany Eubanks-Saunders of Bank of America uses her influence to diversify not only her own team, but also the teams of her non-diverse counterparts. She recalls a situation where her manager's peer was impressed by an accomplished black female banker whom Eubanks-Saunders had introduced him to. When she pressed him as to why he didn't extend an offer to this woman to join his team, he explained he had no open positions. Eubanks-Saunders didn't let him off the hook. "You have inferior talent on your team today that will not be able to continue to add value," she told him. "The same mindset that allows you to consider top-grading talent to hire an impressive non-diverse candidate is the same mindset that you should be willing to use in this instance to hire top talent women and minorities. Hiring her will not only drive higher capacity and results for your team, but will also improve your diverse representation."

Eubanks-Saunders prevailed. The new hire subsequently so exceeded the executive's expectations that she was promoted less than twelve months after she arrived. But Eubanks-Saunders had to push the executive out of his comfort zone because, she points out, he had so little experience with black women as business partners. "Some white men are used to seeing minority women work in less technical roles, or as domestic helpers," she observes. "To expect that they would trust that we could perform at a level that they have not personally witnessed is probably ambitious thinking. That is why it is so important that as black women in positions of business influence, we take the lead to identify high-potential talent, coach and mentor that talent, and not be shy about hiring that talent into the organization."

And while Eubanks-Saunders says that there have been a few times when non-diverse peers have not appreciated her passion, she hasn't experienced any setbacks for providing that sponsorship and exercising that leadership. "I'm no political social activist, by any stretch," she says. "I try to be balanced in my approach and always model a high degree of professionalism, respect, and fairness. However, I do feel that as a leader, I cannot be afraid to share a different perspective: the black perspective. Whenever I see inequity, I am compelled to bring attention to it. Not only is it my personal obligation, but I believe that it is an expectation that Bank of America, with its commitment to diversity and inclusion, has of me as a leader."

CHANGING THE FACE OF LEADERSHIP

Wanting to be in a position to lift up other minority talent in the workplace helps explain why black women want power. But it's also evident that black women, more than white, want to be in a position to tackle inequities and lift up others *outside* of work as well. Forty-two percent (as compared to 27 percent of white women) aspire to make a significant contribution to their communities. Sixty percent aspire to create something meaningful or lasting in their lifetime. A stunning 65 percent (as compared to 34 percent of white women) aspire to be faithful to their religions. These numbers echo those we published in an earlier study called *Leadership in our Midst* (2005): African American women turned out to be far more likely than white men (25 percent vs. 16 percent) to hold pivotal roles in religious communities, and to engage in hands-on social outreach (41 percent vs. 32 percent). They were also far more likely than white women (25 percent vs. 14 percent) to be on the front lines helping young people in their communities as mentors, tutors, and "big sisters." As Ella Bell then observed, "They comprise the backbone of religious organizations and provide a significant part of the energy driving communities in the United States."

From our current study, it's evident they are still this driving force. Joyce Trimuel is a case in point. When she was at Chubb, she shouldered the responsibilities of running the Multicultural Development Council board on top of the formidable profit-and-loss responsibilities of her day job. And yet she found time as well to serve on KIPP, the education initiative that gives inner-city minority students exposure and opportunities they are otherwise not likely to get. Trimuel told us she got as much out of her involvement, as a volunteer leader, as the kids she served did. "We are able to create moments where these kids see people of color go to college and graduate, where they see people like themselves in school, doing well, or in a corporation, running a business," she explains. "To have impact like that is incredibly rewarding; it has made me a better person."

It's hardly surprising that black women who have punched through to the top place such an emphasis on being a role model and mentor: they know just how taxing it is to be the one, the only, or the first. The trailblazer role can get wearisome, our interviewees point out; as one Harvard MBA and twenty-year consulting veteran told us, "I'm tired, and I'm tired of being tired." But what impels these women to keep blazing the trail is realizing that they wouldn't be on it at all if their grandmothers and mothers had given in to their weariness. In the words of our consulting veteran, "For my children, and their children, I can find the strength to open a door for another deserving person of color—just as a person of color found the strength to open it for me."

9

Earning Well

Ten years ago, Trisch Smith took her mother to London, England. It was something of a milestone for both. At twenty-eight, Smith was on track to be named EVP at Edelman, the world's largest public relations firm; at fifty, her mom was making her first international trip with her daughter. "It was one of those moments, the kind I'm always striving for," says Smith. "It was so fulfilling, because it was a return on her investment. She's a third grade teacher and had me in her early twenties; she sacrificed tremendously to ensure I had opportunities she never had. My success is all to do with her, and for her."

Such are the joys of earning well, which, Smith concedes, is one of her top five drivers. And our research shows that Smith, who is black, speaks for most black women: a stunning 81 percent, as compared to 54 percent of their white counterparts, say that earning well is very important in their work or career. A majority (54 percent, as compared to 46 percent of white women) cite financial independence as one of their top three goals currently.

WHY MONEY MATTERS

Citing her own grandmother, a widow who raised, supported, and educated nine children, Tiffany Eubanks-Saunders offers one explanation: "Financial stability was key for not only me, but also for all my college female friends, classmates, and sorority sisters. Growing up with a single parent, working multiple jobs, and still needing a little bit of government assistance is not something that you forget quickly." She adds, "Financial freedom and stability was definitely something we'd talk about as a stated goal of success, because you didn't *ever* want to have to depend on anyone for anything."

Not only are black women absolutely intent on providing for themselves, but many are supporting a constellation of relatives, in part because they feel they owe their success to others, but also because they take considerable joy in spreading their wealth to loved ones. "I've always been our family's primary breadwinner," one black attorney explained, "and I've loved being able to help my own children, not just paying for their education but providing them with opportunities I never had, to travel the world and be exposed to things like music. But I supported my mom until she died, and I supported my brother, who was a schoolteacher, along with his children and grandchildren. I continue to support my church and my schools and several refugee agencies. In fact, pretty much everything and everyone I care about in the world, I give money to." She adds, "It's not something I set out to do, but it's terribly important that I remain in a position to do it."

Making good money is important to all women, but only the black women we interviewed offered no apology for prioritizing it. "Money is a proxy for power in the corporate world," Celeste, the DC-based attorney, told us. "If you want power in a company, you need to fight to be highly compensated. Money means something: it tells people how much the company thinks of you. Even as a little kid I could see that money and power went hand in hand." To be heard, as a black woman, says Celeste, it's very simple: "You've got to be a top earner."

WHITE WOMEN, TOO, WANT TO EARN WELL

White women we interviewed uniformly conceded that high compensation was important; many of them had fought for it. But in contrast to black women, each of them took pains to downplay their interest. They explained to us that money was not how they took their measure. They sought to excel and advance in their careers irrespective of compensation. They did recognize that earning well signaled their worth to others, particularly men. Earning men's respect empowered them to have real impact—which *was* what they most wanted from their careers.

This is not to suggest white women aren't interested in what money can do for their families. They consider financial security important; they consider financial independence critical. They want to earn enough to live comfortably. That 61 percent of white women married or living with a partner in our survey earn at least as much as their spouse or partner may help explain why fully 80 percent consider financial security an important aspect of high compensation; why 76 percent say that financial independence matters; and why 79 percent say that sustaining a comfortable lifestyle is key.

Melissa Arnoldi, senior vice president of Technology Service Strategy and Implementation for AT&T, is a case in point. At the moment her family's sole breadwinner, she aspires to be a leader in a Fortune 100 firm, ideally as president of a large business unit. It's the opportunity to have a broader role—one with profit-and-loss responsibility—that appeals to her, as do the visibility and impact such a role would give her. She sees the position surrounding her with great coworkers, and supporting her with a network of strong relationships. But compensation, she emphasizes, is among her motivators for two reasons. She wants the things money can buy: a beach house, more travel overseas, an Ivy League education for her children, health care for her aging parents. And she wants the time it can buy, in the form of an early retirement, so she can do more of what gives her pleasure: travel abroad, spend time in Napa, and give back more to her church, where she feels she could "share her learnings" to inspire girls and young professional women as they embark on their careers. "I enjoy my job, but pay is important," she notes.

Others we have interviewed make clear that they enjoy what an executive salary makes possible. One CEO told us she delights in the "lovely lifestyle" her top job has enabled, from good schools for her children and nice holidays for the family to helping out her parents and setting up her husband in his own business. Another global leader said she loves having the wherewithal to completely renovate her home and take herself on a three-and-a-half week trek to Mount Everest's base camp. The newly appointed director of a cosmetics business described how liberating it is, now that she makes good money, to be "a little careless" in her spending. "I'm glad I'm bringing in money because we tend to enjoy it a lot," she says. "We try not to deny ourselves things that we enjoy, like vacations and travel, or going out to eat, or buying something we think we'll enjoy as a family. We want to be living well today."

WITH ARRIVAL COME ANXIETIES

Our qualitative findings point to an interesting trend among successful women, both black and white: by dint of their success climbing the corporate ladder, they come to assume the role of primary or sole breadwinner. For those with children, and even those without, this can mean ceding domestic responsibilities to their husband or partner.

Sarah, for example, the telecommunications VP who is white, describes how her job responsibilities dictated a reallocation of responsibilities on the home front. "It was a hard decision for my husband to quit his job," she observes, "but it was the right decision for us. Having support at home and the support of my senior leaders has really helped me say, 'I can do this [high-powered job].'"

Similarly, Desiree Ralls-Morrison, who is black, acknowledges that the downside of becoming lead counsel for Boehringer Ingelheim was uprooting her husband and two boys from their home in Philadelphia to follow her to Ridgefield, Connecticut. "When I put the house on the market," she says, "the enormity of it all—from needing to sell the house, and trying to find another; and my husband having to give notice; and the boys going to a new school, all because I wanted this— was overwhelming. It all hit home," she says. "But I never thought it wasn't worth it. I am convinced that it's best for my family, ultimately, for a number of reasons, including greater long-term financial security. And I'm happier—which drives benefits for all of us."

Being the sole or primary breadwinner is not new terrain for black women. But being in a position of leadership, and looking to partners for support at home, is new for both white women and black. And it is potentially revolutionary, as Liza Mundy documents in her book, *The Richer Sex: How the New Majority of Female Breadwinners Is Transforming Sex, Love and Family.* The main concern—one large enough to prompt *The Atlantic, The New York Times* and *The Washington Post* to provide feature coverage, and *TIME* magazine to commission her to write a cover story—is that the crumbling of this gender norm will undermine marital bliss and sabotage domestic peace. Mundy's interviews reveal "breadwomen" to be anxious about the fate of their marriages, given that women who earn more than 60 percent of their household's income are more likely to wind up divorced.[76] But she also shows how the shift in earning power liberates women in their choice of a mate. After all, when men's earning potential is no longer a factor in their eligibility as mates, many more men qualify as marriage material.[77]

We uncovered concern among high-earning women for their relationships, but that concern did not translate into ambivalence about a high-paying job. A cosmetics business director we interviewed, whose salary in the last year or so has exceeded her husband's, says she is "on the alert" for any changes in the family dynamic but isn't overly worried about the new dynamic, as her recent promotion puts her and her husband, who is ten years older, on more equal footing. "It's sort of like I've caught up with him," she says. "I certainly think that for me, one reason why I wanted to become a director is because there is a pretty steep curve there in terms of income."

And while we expected women who out-earn their spouses or partners to affirm that doing so had thrown their relationship into turmoil, our survey data fails to corroborate our hypothesis: only 1 percent of women who are married, engaged, or living with a partner say that their earning power undermines their marriage/ partnership. Mundy may well be correct in visualizing a future where women not only command the bigger paycheck, but also shrug off to willing partners the bulk of domestic responsibilities.

Because, as the cosmetics director observes, it's her husband who is gunning for her to reach for the C-suite. "I think having someone else who is interested in your accomplishments and gives you positive feedback makes you more aware that the progress you've made is kind of cool," she says. "I've started to think, maybe the only thing standing in my way is me."

EPILOGUE

Where We Go From Here

Feminism is in renaissance. According to a poll conducted by *The Washington Post* and Kaiser Family Foundation in 2015, a robust 68 percent of women say that there is still a need for a strong women's movement today, an endorsement of feminism given by only 48 percent of all women surveyed in 2005 (by CBS News). [78] Nearly as many Millennials (63 percent) identify as feminists as do Boomers (68 percent), and fully 83 percent of these young women (born after 1981) describe feminism as empowering—a word that only 56 percent of women ages sixty-five and older choose.

But, as the 2016 presidential race has made abundantly clear, the next generation of professional women define feminism rather differently than did their forebears. New Wave feminism "is shaped less by a shared struggle against oppression than by a collective embrace of individual freedoms, concerned less with targeting narrowly defined enemies than with broadening feminism's reach," explain the authors of an article based on *The Washington Post* poll's findings. Today, feminists are bound together "not by a handful of national organizations and charismatic leaders but by the invisible bonds of the Internet and social media."[79]

In a word, feminism today is more inclusive. Businesswoman Carly Fiorina considers herself one; so does entertainer Beyoncé. Black feminists like Keisha Zollar, an actress and comedian who likes the term "womanist" because it was coined by women of color, share the tent with white activists like Mindy Finn, the founder and president of Empowered Women. Muslim feminists like Sabin Ahmed, a consultant with the World Bank who believes abortion should be legal in all cases, share the tent with Christian feminists like Charlene McField, a stay-at-home mother who feels abortion should be illegal in all cases.[80]

In becoming more diffuse, feminism is in some ways becoming the inclusive tent it never quite achieved. Because young women are so much more likely to identify as not simply women, but as individuals defined by the intersections between gender and generation, race, religion, sexual orientation, and socioeconomic status, they are acutely conscious that Friedan's feminism only spoke to white women privileged enough to be housewives. With 43 percent of all Millennials in the US identifying as non-white, the next wave of the women's movement is fundamentally more inclined to see the fight for equal rights as encompassing more than gender discrimination. [81] Indeed, while 85 percent of women think there's a lot of or some discrimination against women, just as many think there's a lot of or some discrimination against African Americans (84 percent) and gays and lesbians (85 percent).[82] Addressing income inequality as it threatens to undermine the American social contract is as urgent, if not more so, than solving for the inequities suffered by women.

Nowhere has this evolution in feminism been made more evident than in the run-up to the 2016 presidential election. To the horror of First and Second Wave feminists, many New Wavers favored presidential candidate Bernie Sanders over Hillary Clinton. "There's a special place in hell for women who don't help each other," former (and first female) Secretary of State Madeline Albright told New Hampshire primary voters, urging them to back Clinton to win the broader fight for equality.[83] Gloria Steinem went one step further, suggesting to Bill Maher on his talk show before the first primary that young women were flocking to the Sanders camp because they were looking to meet boys.[84] But such remarks only underscored, for younger women voters, how deep and wide yawns the chasm between their feminism and their mothers'. Hillary Clinton, to women at the intersections, represents a movement that was exclusive of women of color, gay and lesbian women, and poor or uneducated women. To them, Hillary Clinton utterly embodies the white, privileged bra-burners who saw men as the barrier to their ambitions and the cause of their oppression. As nineteen-year old Caela Camazine, a freshman at Penn State intent on becoming a doctor, explained to *The New*

York Times, electing Hillary might open the door to a shift in pronouns for doctors (from "he/him" to "she/her")—but Camazine was backing Sanders because his emphasis on fighting inequality mirrored more closely her values as a feminist.[85]

United in their belief that feminism is about having choices, young women are eager to choose their own paths toward happiness, whether that means pursuing a career, raising children, being active in their communities, starting a business, making the world a better place, or some combination of all these aspirations. Conscious that their mothers and grandmothers blazed trails through very different landscapes, black women and white women today are rightfully leery of canned advice from women who preceded them in the workplace.

We would be remiss, however, if we didn't channel some of the considerable wisdom these history makers and trail blazers offer up to New Wavers as they pass the baton. Because, for all of the ways in which the path forward differs for black women and white, some challenges remain the same; and for all the ways in which the past differentiates their experience, some aspects of being female cross all divides, including race and generation. As both Mary Jean Collins, the seventy-five-year-old former National Organization for Women leader, and Jenny Jaffe, the twenty-six-year-old comedian and founder of Project UROK, acknowledge, much work remains to be done, however individually and uniquely women go about doing it. "Do we NOT need feminism anymore?" challenges Jaffe. "F— THAT! Yeah, we need feminism! We need feminism until ALL women are equal!"[86]

WORDS FROM THE WISE
Advice for Ambitious Women

CULTIVATE A SPONSOR

A tremendous piece of luck as well as hard work and focus put me within striking distance of getting this very fancy Kennedy Scholarship, the British memorial to JFK, at Harvard. It was in a way the British equivalent of the Rhodes, and it was only in its second year when I heard about it. I happened to know someone who got it the first year. He said, "Look, go and apply, because if you want to go to the States, this is really the way to do it." So then I really sank my teeth into becoming a good candidate. Without something like that scholarship, it would have been very difficult to bring off a move to the States because I clearly didn't have the connections or family money that would have allowed me to come as a grad student. I wouldn't have known how to do it. I was powerless to do it.

But I was pretty good at passing exams—and, even more importantly, I had a sponsor in my sights. Her name was Jean Grove. She was my tutor at Cambridge, had supervised my studies and saw me as both capable and ambitious in a way that the more precious upper-middle-class girls were not. I wasn't at all conflicted about success. I knew that no one in the world was going to solve my life for me. I had to do it myself, and I had to do something powerful with my life. I wanted to earn money and be a professional.

Dr. Grove *really* went to bat for me. At the end of my second year at Cambridge, she offered me a research position with her team in Africa, guided me to grants that I could use to pay my way, and then wrote recommendations for me to get those grants. She and I spent the whole summer doing research in Ghana. And we wrote an article together, so I had a published piece of scholarly work.

Jean very cleverly gave me the opportunities that allowed me to shine and which set me up for success. She allowed me to become deeply involved in African development at a time when decolonization was going on. It was a very alluring thing that I'd done, working in Ghana and publishing work about it. In terms of my winning the Kennedy Scholarship, it was likely the breakthrough qualification.

So when I came to Harvard, in a sense the world was at my feet. I had left behind the whole class thing: no one understood the significance of coming from the town I'd come from. I had an enormous number of opportunities. And were it not for Jean's sponsorship I'd have had none of them.

—Sylvia Ann Hewlett

SPEAK YOUR TRUTH, ACCEPT ITS CONSEQUENCES

I had opportunities at the bank, but I was never naïve enough to think I had the same opportunities as my white counterparts because I didn't. I remember having a conversation with a colleague of mine in HR about a female peer. I was doing what I thought was good work, but I could see—we had access to everyone's pay information—that she was getting raises, not me. That wasn't happening all the time, but I did experience it, as did other black women. As good as our work was, you just didn't see African American women rise in the firm. Still today there are plenty of firms where you don't see African American women, let alone in leadership. That kind of discrimination hasn't gone away.

Which is why, forty-five years later, I tell my daughter and daughter in law to be conscious of their choices. You always have a choice, to be bold or not. Are you okay *not* saying what you really think? There's no right or wrong answer to that; just know what you want and then be willing to bear the consequences of your decision, as I was. I'd give my point of view when people asked for it, and that may have impacted me in my career progression. But I was okay with that. The question for black women, maybe all women: are you willing to step out? Because there will be consequences, and you need to be okay with that.

—Geri Thomas

ASPIRE TO EARN WELL

I became conscious as I was going to *Marie Claire* that there was this whole generation of women who really weren't being spoken to in terms of their ambitions for a really big life. It felt like we were re-entering a moment where women could have it all. The idea of the father arriving home on the 5:52 to be greeted by his wife with a martini and not talking to his children—that era was gone.

And yet the new normal is a tough place to be. Many women have extreme jobs. They're facing a lot of insecurity. Pay has plateaued. It's not an easy universe out there.

So it's important to remind women how incredibly thrilling it is to be independent, how incredibly empowering it is to have a sense of control over your own life—and how incredibly liberating it is to have a little fund of money that you have saved up, so that if you don't like what you're doing you can turn around to the boss and say, "Thanks, but I am going to try something else."

We don't talk about this enough. We talk about sex, but we don't talk about money. We don't talk to women enough about how very, very stressful it is to be in debt, to be pulled apart financially. A whole generation of girls is graduating right now who are going to be substantially in debt from college loans. You see people going off to grad school to get an MFA and racking up another sixty thousand dollars of debt. It is very stressful paying that money back and I think women forget that.

At *Cosmo*, we tell women to pursue a career because a good income buys you freedom. It buys you freedom from bosses that you no longer want to work with. It buys you freedom from a miserable relationship. It buys you choices and opportunities. You can go to Paris for the weekend. You can buy yourself a Gucci bag that you have always fantasized about. You can dress the part. You can buy your own apartment, you can buy your own car, you can buy a house in the country. You can make choices for your children, to send them to camp, to private school, to college. These are all real life decisions that, if you earn money, are really enjoyable to make. The freedom to be able to do all that, to have those choices and opportunities, is incredibly nice. And regardless of whether you are married or not, incredibly important.

—Joanna Coles

PERSEVERE—BUT ASK FOR HELP

The roles of men and women have changed dramatically. Men are more involved in their families, which is good for them, their children, and their wives. Women are in the world of work, many in nontraditional roles, and are seen as very competitive. The thought that it was okay to pay women less because men were breadwinners is now seen as anachronistic.

In fact, there's a new gender gap: lots of very talented women in their thirties are single-minded in their focus on career success, just as men once were. Younger black women are taking no prisoners. They're setting goals, and they're reaching them. But women's new roles, especially as they strive for leadership, put great strains on family and relationships. Women are finding themselves compromised in many ways as wives and mothers.

So you have to have resolve. Set some goals. Decide you want to achieve them, and have confidence in your own decision. Know that people will try, for various reasons, to hold you back. They'll say, "You're too ambitious, start lower!" or, "You ought to get married first," or "Let your brother go first." Say to yourself, "I can do this." Be aware that at times, people's motives in holding you back may have more to do with their own feelings about a lack of progress, and wanting not to be outdistanced.

Success is all about resolve. Surround yourself with people who can help you find it, and keep it, along the way. If you are not sure how to meet your goals, don't be afraid to ask others for help. When people see you persevering toward your goals with determination, many will be inclined to reach out to help you.

—Charlene Drew Jarvis, PhD

FIND YOUR SISTERHOOD

I have a few friends who are dear to me. If we're addressing each other, we call each other sister. That's how I feel toward them. Sisterhood is extraordinarily important, especially for women as they go about tackling sexism and racism. You have to have your go-to people, in groups, in numbers, that will support, comfort, and challenge you. You need a circle of women who will do that for you in your life.

My friends are feminists alongside me. We're talking through these issues and thinking how, together, we can support each other. Sheryl Sandberg, COO of Facebook, is one of my closest friends, along with Michelle Kydd Lee, chief innovation officer for Creative Artists Agency, and Dambisa Moyo, global economist. Where these women are and what they've managed to do, in different ways in different industries, is extraordinary. We feel aligned, all of us, around our responsibility to each other and to the broader community of women, even though we're living and doing our thing in different ways both spoken and unspoken.

And that support is unconditional. Sisterhood is super important. You've got to have go-to people whom you can trust when things get really tough. Because we all are going to have really bad moments during our careers.

—Mellody Hobson

ENDNOTES

1. Betty Friedan, *The Feminine Mystique* (New York: WW Norton & Co., 1963), 32.

2. Estelle B. Freedman, *No Turning Back: The History of Feminism and the Future of Women* (New York: Balantine Books, 2002).

3. bell hooks, *Feminist Theory: From Margin to Center,* 2nd Ed. (London: Pluto Press, 2000), 2.

4. "Founding: Setting the Stage," National Organization for Women, July 2006, http://now.org/about/history /founding-2/; Rebecca Tara-Lee, "The Power of Female Friendship in Chicago," July 1, 2015, http://fw-chicago.com /profiles/influencers/the -power-of-female-friendship-in-chicago/; Beverly Guy-Sheftall, ed., *Words of Fire: An Anthology of African-American Feminist Thought* (New York: The New Press, 2011), Kindle edition, 15.

5. Becky Thompson, "Multiracial Feminism: Recasting the Chronology of Second Wave Feminism," *Feminist Studies* (2002): 337-36, doi: 10.2307/3178747; Guy-Sheftall, *Words of Fire,* 1-22 (see note 4).

6. Jane Kramer, "Road Warrior," *The New Yorker*, October 19, 2015, http://www.newyorker.com/magazine/2015 /10/19/road -warrior-profiles-jane-kramer.

7. Amy Jacques Garvey, "Our Women Getting into the Larger Life," in *Words of Fire: An Anthology of African-American Feminist Thought* ed. Beverly Guy-Sheftall (New York: The New Press, 2011), Kindle edition, 93-94.

8. Ibid.

9. Sojourner Truth, "'Ain't I a Woman?' December 1851," Internet Modern History Sourcebook: Paul Halsall, August 1997, https:// legacy.fordham.edu/halsall/mod/sojtruth-woman.asp.

10. Jacqueline Jones, *Labor of Love, Labor of Sorrow: Black Women, Work, and the Family, from Slavery to the Present* (New York: Basic Books, 2010), 198.

11. Shonda Rhimes, *Year of Yes: How to Dance it Out, Stand in the Sun, and Be Your Own Person* (New York: Simon & Schuster, 2015).

12. Doris Weatherford, *American Women and World War II* (Edison, NJ: Castle Books, 2008).

13. Claudia D. Goldin, "The Role of World War II in the Rise of Women's Employment," *The American Economic Review* 81, no. 4 (1991): 741–56, http://www.jstor.org/stable/2006640.

14. Friedan, *The Feminine Mystique,* 22 (see note 1).

15. William Hamilton Harris, *The Harder We Run: Black Workers Since The Civil War* (New York: Oxford University Press, 1982), 113-122.

16. Karen Tucker Anderson, "Last Hired, First Fired: Black Women Workers During World War II," *The Journal of American History* 69, no. 1 (1982): 82-97, doi: 10.2307/1887753.

17. Maya Angelou, *I Know Why The Caged Bird Sings* (New York: Random House, 1969), 268-269.

18. Jones, *Labor of Love, Labor of Sorrow*, 203 (see note 10).

19. Anderson, "Last Hired, First Fired," 89 (see note 16).

20. In 1950, 30 percent of black wives with husbands continued to work, compared to 19 percent of white wives (Jones, *Labor of Love, Labor of Sorrow*, 216, 222 (see note 10); Glen G. Cain, *Married Women in the Labor Force: An Economic Analysis* (Chicago: University of Chicago, 1966)).

21. *Poverty in the United States 1959 to 1968,* prepared by the United States Department of Commerce (Washington, DC: US Department of Commerce, 1975), https://www.census.gov /hhes/www/poverty/publications/p60-68a.pdf.

22. Despite the institution of Title VII, which proscribes discrimination based on sex, race, color, national origin, and religion in employment, households headed by black women in 1968 were more than two times as likely to exist below the poverty line as households headed by white women (*Poverty in the United States*, USDOC (see note 22)).

23. Restitution for lost wages to slaves—estimated at $2 to $4 trillion—gives only the most superficial sense of the economic devastation wreaked on black families due to slavery. These lost wages do not take into consideration the losses incurred by the inability of black men and women to hold property; to own or invest in businesses; or to obtain certifications in various

professions, such as law or medicine. Long after the end of slavery, black men and women continued to face discrimination in areas critical to wealth accumulation, such as property ownership and professional certification, due in no small part to Jim Crow Laws (Melvin L. Oliver and Thomas M. Shapiro, *Black Wealth, White Wealth: A New Perspective on Racial Inequality* (New York: Taylor & Francis, 2006), 3-4; Dalton Conley, "The Cost of Slavery," *New York Times,* February 15, 2003, http://www .nytimes.com/2003/02/15 /opinion/the-cost-of-slavery.html).

24. David Cooper, Mary Gable, and Algernon Austin, *The Public-Sector Jobs Crisis: Women and African Americans Hit Hardest by Job Losses in State and Local Governments* (Washington DC: Economic Policy Institute, 2012), http://www.epi.org/files /2012 /bp339-public-sector-jobs-crisis.pdf.

25. William B. Harvey, Adia M. Harvey, and Mark King, "The Impact of the Brown v. Board of Education Decision on Postsecondary Participation of African Americans," *The Journal of Negro Education* 73, no. 3 (2004): doi: 10.2307/4129615.

26. In the wake of Title VII, there was a more than 100 percent increase in the percentage of black women in clerical jobs—from 10 percent to 22 percent of black women (Bart Landry, *The New Black Middle Class* (Berkeley: University of California Press, 1987), 90).

27. Irene Padavic and Barbara F. Reskin, *Women and Men at Work* (London: Pine Forge Press, 2002), 55-56.

28. Russell Sage Foundation, "The Rise of Women: Seven Charts Showing Women's Rapid Gains in Educational Achievement," (New York: Russell Sage Foundation, February 21, 2013), http://www.russellsage.org/blog/rise -women-seven-charts -showing-womens-rapid-gains-educational-achievement.

29. Jo Freeman, "Shirley Chisholm's 1972 Presidential Race," February 2005, http://www.uic.edu /orgs/cwluherstory /jofreeman/polhistory/chisholm.htm; see also Richard L. Madden, "Mrs. Chisholm Defeats Farmer, Is First Negro Woman in House; First Negro Woman Wins House Seat," *New York Times,* November 6, 1968, http://query.nytimes.com/mem/archive /pdf?res=9502EFDE1F3BE73ABC4E53DFB7678383679EDE.

30. "Coretta Scott King: About Mrs. King," The King Center, 2014, http://www.thekingcenter.org/about-mrs-king.

31. "The Nobel Prize in Literature 1993," The Nobel Foundation, http://www.nobelprize.org/nobel_prizes/literature/laureates /1993/; See, for example, Toni Morrison, *The Bluest Eye,* 1970; Maya Angelou, *I Know Why the Caged Bird Sings,* 1969; Alice Walker, *The Color Purple,* 1982.

32. Judith Warner, "Fact Sheet: The Women's Leadership Gap," The Center for American Progress, March 7, 2014, https://www .americanprogress.org/issues/women/report/2014/03/07 /85457/fact-sheet-the-womens-leadership-gap/.

33. "The World's 100 Most Powerful Women: #29 Ursula Burns," *Forbes,* 2015, http://www.forbes.com/profile /ursula-burns/.

34. Kimberlé W. Crenshaw, "Justice Rising: Moving Intersectionally in the Age of Post-Everything," London School of Economics, March 26, 2014, http://www.lse.ac.uk/newsAndMedia/videoAndAudio /channels/publicLecturesAndEvents/player.aspx?id=2360.

35. Kimberlé Crenshaw, "Demarginalizing the Intersection of Race and Sex: A Black Feminist Critique of Antidiscrimination Doctrine, Feminist Theory and Antiracist Politics," *University of Chicago Legal Forum* (1989): 139-167, http://chicagounbound.uchicago .edu/cgi/viewcontent.cgi?article=1052&context=uclf.

36. Women of color hold just 3.2 percent of board seats of Fortune 500 companies, and more than two thirds of Fortune 500 companies have no women of color as board directors at all (Warner, "Fact Sheet" (see note 32)).

37. Crenshaw, "Justice Rising" (see note 34).

38. Bill Bradley, "Mellody Hobson," *TIME,* 2015, http://time.com /3822587/mellody-hobson-2015-time-100/.

39. Liz Welch, "What Do You Do if You're Sexually Assaulted Abroad," *Cosmopolitan Magazine,* December 8, 2014, http://www .cosmopolitan.com/politics/news/a33996/sexual-assault -abroad/; Sara Austin, "How Not to Get Pregnant: The Cosmo Guide to Contraception," *Cosmopolitan Magazine,* August 14, 2013, http://www .cosmopolitan.com/sex-love /advice/a4673/cosmo-guide-to-contraception/.

40. "Ellie Awards Winners and Finalists Database," *American Society of Magazine Editors*, 2015, http://www .cosmopolitan.com /sex-love/advice/a4673/cosmo-guide-to-contraception/.

41. Warner, "Fact Sheet" (see note 32).

42. Mellody Hobson, "Exclusive Book Excerpt: Own Who You Are," *Essence Magazine*, April 7, 2014, http://www .essence.com/2014 /04/07/exclusive-book-excerpt-own-who-you-are

43. Eighty-Eighth Congress of the United States, *Civil Rights Act of 1964*, National Archives Catalog (Washington DC: 1964), https:// catalog.archives.gov/id/299891.

44. Alan Hughes, "75 Most Powerful Blacks on Wall Street," *Black Enterprise*, November 7, 2011, http://www.blackenterprise.com /mag/75-most-powerful-blacks-on-wall-street-2/13/.

45. "Women in the United States," Catalyst, June 10, 2014, http:// www.catalyst.org/knowledge/women-united-states.

46. The Association to Advance Collegiate Schools of Business, "Women's Share of MBAs Earned in the US," Catalyst, 2014, http://www.catalyst.org/knowledge/womens-share-mbas -earned-us; Widget Finn, "MBA Women: Breaking Down Barriers at Business School," *The Telegraph*, November 22, 2012, http://www.telegraph.co.uk /education/educationadvice/9683856 /MBA-women-breaking-down-barriers-at-business-school.html.

47. Sylvia Ann Hewlett, Melinda Marshall, and Laura Sherbin, with Tara Gonsalves, *Innovation, Diversity and Market Growth* (New York: Center for Talent Innovation, 2013).

48. Unpublished data from Sylvia Ann Hewlett, Noni Allwood, Karen Sumberg, and Sandra Scharf, with Christina Fargnoli, *Cracking the Code: Executive Presence and Multicultural Professionals* (New York: Center for Talent Innovation: 2013).

49. Sylvia Ann Hewlett, Maggie Jackson, and Ellis Cose, with Courtney Emerson, *Vaulting the Color Bar: How Sponsorship Levers Multicultural Professionals into Leadership* (New York: Center for Talent Innovation, 2012).

50. Ibid.

51. *Ambition and Gender at Work*, Institute of Leadership & Management (London: Institute of Leadership and Management, 2011), https://www.i-l-m.com/~/media/ILM%20Website /Downloads/Insight/Reports_from_ILM_website/ILM_Ambition _and_Gender_report_0211%20pdf.ashx.

52. Zachary Estes and Sydney Felker, "Confidence Mediates the Sex Difference in Mental Rotation Performance," *Archive of Sexual*

Behavior 41, no. 3 (2012): 557-70, doi:10.1007/s10508-011 -9875-5.

53. Katty Kay and Claire Shipman, *The Confidence Code: The Science and Art of Self-Assurance—What Women Should Know* (New York: HarperCollins, 2014).

54. Patricia Sellers, "Power: Do Women Really Want It?" *Fortune,* October 13, 2003, http://archive.fortune.com/magazines /fortune/fortune_archive/2003/10/13/350932/index.htm.

55. Anne-Marie Slaughter, "Why Women Still Can't Have It All," The *Atlantic,* July/August 2012, http://www.theatlantic.com /magazine/archive/2012/07/why-women-still-cant-have-it -all/309020/.

56. Katherine Boyle, "Atlantic Magazine Story Goes Viral, and Women Have Something to Say About Having 'It All,'" *Washington Post,* June 24, 2012, https://www.washingtonpost .com/lifestyle/style/atlantic-story-on-whether-women-could -have-it-all/2012/06/24/gJQAihWQ0V_story.html.

57. Indra Nooyi, interview with David Bradley, *Can Women Have It All?,* The Aspen Institute, July 3, 2014, YouTube Video, starting at 21:17, https://www.youtube.com/watch?v=KzLpryLUYsk.

58. Arianna Huffington, *Thrive: The Third Metric to Redefining Success and Creating a Life of Well-Being, Wisdom, and Wonder* (New York: Harmony Books, 2014).

59. Sylvia Ann Hewlett and Melinda Marshall, *Women Want Five Things* (New York: Center for Talent Innovation, 2014).

60. Sylvia Ann Hewlett, with Kerrie Peraino, Laura Sherbin, and Karen Sumberg, *The Sponsor Effect: Breaking Through the Last Glass Ceiling* (Cambridge: Harvard Business Review, 2010); Sylvia Ann Hewlett, Melinda Marshall, and Laura Sherbin, with Barbara Adachi, *Sponsor Effect 2.0: Road Maps for Sponsors and Protégés* (New York: Center for Talent Innovation, 2012).

61. Ibid.

62. Hewlett et al., *Sponsor Effect 2.0,* 26-7 (see note 60).

63. Hewlett et al., *Vaulting the Color Bar* (see note 49).

64. Sylvia Ann Hewlett, Lauren Leader-Chiveé, Laura Sherbin, and Joanne Gordon, with Fabiola Dieudonné, *Executive Presence* (New York: Center for Talent Innovation, 2012).

65. Unpublished data from Hewlett et al., *Cracking the Code* (see note 48).

66. Hewlett et al., *Sponsor Effect 2.0* (see note 60).

67. Robert A. Karasek, "Job Demands, Job Decision Latitude, and Mental Strain: Implications for Job Redesign," *Administrative Science Quarterly* 24, no. 2 (1979): 285-308, http://www.jstor .org/stable/2392498?seq=1#page_scan_tab_contents.

68. Paul A. Landsbergis, "Occupational Stress Among Health Care Workers: A Test of the Job Demands-Control Model," *Journal of Organizational Behavior* 9, no. 3 (1988): 217-239, doi:10.1002/job.4030090303; Kevin Daniels and Andrew Guppy, "Occupational Stress, Social Support, Job Control, and Psychological Well-Being," *Human Relations* 47, no. 12 (1994): 1523-1544, doi: 10.1177/001872679404701205; Pascale Carayon, "A Longitudinal Test of Karasek's Job Strain Model among Office Workers," *Work and Stress* 7, no. 4 (1993): 299-314, doi:10.1080/02678379308257070; Toby D. Wall, et al., "The Demands-Control Model of Job Strain: A More Specific Test," *Journal of Occupational and Organizational Psychology* 69, no. 2 (1996): 153-166, doi:10.1111/j.2044-8325.1996.tb00607.x.

69. Shirley Fisher, "Control and Blue Collar Work" in *Job Stress and Blue Collar Work* (Chichester: John Wiley & Sons, 1985).

70. Bruce S. McEwen, "Physiology and Neurobiology of Stress and Adaptation: Central Role of the Brain," *Physiological Reviews* 87, no. 3 (2007): 873-904, http://www.ncbi.nlm.nih.gov/pubmed /17615391.

71. Anna Fels, *Necessary Dreams: Ambition in Women's Changing Lives* (New York: Pantheon Books, 2004); Robert Winthrop White, *Lives in Progress: A Study of the Natural Growth of Personality* (Austin: Holt, Rinehart and Winston, 1966).

72. Anna Fels, "Do Women Lack Ambition?" *Harvard Business Review*, April 2004, https://hbr.org/2004/04/do-women-lack -ambition.

73. "#92 Risa Lavizzo-Mourey," *Forbes*, accessed March 22, 2016, http://www.forbes.com/profile/risa-lavizzo-mourey/.

74. Sylvia Ann Hewlett, Carolyn Buck Luce, Lisa J. Servon, Laura Sherbin, Peggy Shiller, Eytan Sosnovich, and Karen Sumberg, *The*

Athena Factor: Reversing the Brain Drain in Science, Engineering, and Technology (Cambridge: Harvard Business Review, 2008).

75. Sylvia Ann Hewlett, Laura Sherbin, Fabiola Dieudonné, Christina Fargnoli, and Catherine Fredman, *Athena Factor 2.0: Accelerating Female Talent in Science, Engineering & Technology* (New York: Center for Talent Innovation, 2014).

76. Liza Mundy, *The Richer Sex: How the New Majority of Female Breadwinners is Transforming Sex, Love and Family* (New York: Simon & Shuster, 2012), 90.

77. Ibid, 92.

78. "Washington Post-Kaiser Family Foundation poll – Feminism in the US," *Washington Post*, June 2015, https://www .washingtonpost.com/apps/g/page/national/washington-post -kaiser-family-foundation-poll-feminism-in-the-us/1946/.

79. Dave Sheinin, Krissah Thompson, Soraya Nadia McDonald, and Scott Clement, "Betty Friedan to Beyoncé: Today's Generation Embraces Feminism on Its Own Terms," *Washington Post*, January 27, 2016, https://www.washingtonpost.com/national /feminism/betty-friedan-to-beyonce-todays-generation -embraces-feminism-on-its-own-terms/2016/01/27/ab480e74 -8e19-11e5-ae1f-af46b7df8483_story.html.

80. "What Type of Feminist (or Anti-Feminist) Are You?" *Washington Post*, January 21, 2016, https://www.washingtonpost.com/graphics /national/feminism-project/feminism-typology-quiz/?tid=a_inl.

81. "Millennials in Adulthood," Pew Research Center, March 7, 2014, http://www.pewsocialtrends.org/2014/03/07/millennials-in -adulthood/.

82. "Washington Post-Kaiser Family Foundation poll – Feminism in the US," *Washington Post*, June 2015, https://www. washingtonpost.com/apps/g/page/national/washington-post -kaiser-family-foundation-poll-feminism-in-the-us/1946/.

83. Alan Rappeport, "Gloria Steinem and Madeleine Albright Rebuke Young Women Backing Bernie Sanders," *New York Times*, February 7, 2016, http://www.nytimes.com/2016/02/08/us /politics/gloria-steinem-madeleine-albright-hillary-clinton -bernie-sanders.html?_r=0.

84. Ibid.

85. Sheryl Gay Stolberg, "Hillary Clinton's Candidacy Reveals Generational Schism among Women," *New York Times,* February 16, 2016, http://www.nytimes.com/2016/02/17/us/hillary -clintons-candidacy-reveals-generational-schism-among-women .html?_r=1.

86. "What Type of Feminist" *Washington Post* (see note 80).

METHODOLOGY

The research consists of a survey, Insights In-Depth® sessions (a proprietary web-based tool used to conduct voice-facilitated virtual focus groups) involving more than sixty-five people from our Task Force organizations, and one-on-one interviews with seventy-two men and women in the US.

The national survey was conducted online in June 2014 among 3,298 respondents (1,578 men and 1,720 women with 788 white women and 356 black women) between the ages of twenty-one and sixty-four currently employed in certain white-collar occupations, with at least a bachelor's degree. Data were weighted to be representative of the US population on key demographics (age, sex, race/ethnicity, region, education, and income). The base used for statistical testing was the effective base.

The survey was conducted by Knowledge Networks under the auspices of the Center for Talent Innovation, a non-profit research organization. Knowledge Networks was responsible for the data collection, while the Center for Talent Innovation conducted the analysis.

ACKNOWLEDGMENTS

The authors are deeply grateful to the sponsors of this research—American Express, AT&T, Bank of America, Boehringer Ingelheim USA, Chubb, The Depository Trust & Clearing Corporation, Intel, Merck KGaA,* The Moody's Foundation, Morgan Stanley, and White & Case LLP—for their generous support. We would also like to thank the cochairs of the Task Force for Talent Innovation—Redia Anderson, Erika Irish Brown, Cynthia Bowman, Deb Bubb, Yrthya Dinzey-Flores, Deborah Elam, Gail Fierstein, Cassandra Frangos, Trevor Gandy, David Gonzales, Wanda Hope, Rosalind Hudnell, Renee Johnson, Patricia Langer, Keri Matthews, Chris Meyrick, Kendall O'Brien, Lisa Garcia Quiroz, Craig Robinson, Shari Slate, Sarah St. Clair, David Tamburelli, Eileen Taylor, Karyn Twaronite, Anilu Vazquez-Ubarri, Anré Williams, and Melinda Wolfe—for their vision and commitment.

We deeply appreciate the efforts of the CTI team, specifically Noni Allwood, Justin Bilyeu, Joseph Cervone, Kennedy Ihezie, Julia Taylor Kennedy, Peggy Shiller, and Jennifer Zephirin. Thanks also to Terri Chung, Danielle Cruz, Colin Elliot, Mark Fernandez,

---

* Darmstadt, Germany

Jessica Jia, Lawrence Jones, Joan Snyder Kuhl, Carolyn Buck Luce, Deidra Mascoll, Rebecca Midura, Andrea Turner Moffitt, Ripa Rashid, Brandon Urquhart, and Eunice Yu for their support. We also appreciate the support provided by our interns Roxanna Azari and Thomas Tuthill.

Thanks to the private sector members of the Task Force for Talent Innovation for their practical ideas and collaborative energy: Elaine Aarons, Rachael Akohonae, Jennifer Allyn, Rohini Anand, Jolen Anderson, Renee Anderson, Michelle Angier, Diane Ashley, Nadine Augusta, Jane Ayaduray, Ken Barrett, Tony Byers, Myrna Chao, Kenneth Charles, Jyoti Chopra, Elise Clarke, Janessa Cox, Fiona Daniel, Nancy Di Dia, Nicole Erb, Hedieh Fakhriyazdi, Grace Figueredo, Kent Gardiner, Heide Gardner, Marc Grainger, Lisa Gutierrez, Kathleen Hart, Linda Hartman-Reehl, Neesha Hathi, Clare Hawthorne, Maja Hazell, Jessica Heffron, Kara Helander, Celia Pohani Huber, Bill Huffaker, Sylvia James, Panagiotis (Pete) Karahalios, Barbara Keen, Shannon Kelleher, Rosemarie Lanard, Frances G. Laserson, Maja Lehnus, Janice Little, Cynthia Marshall, Beth McCormick, Mark McLane, Piyush Mehta, Sylvester Mendoza, Michele Meyer-Shipp, Carolanne Minashi, Kristen Mleczko, Loren Monroe-Trice, Meredith Moore, Christal Morris, Leena Nair, Janell Nelson, Birgit Neu, Elizabeth Nieto, Pamela Norley, Jennifer O'Lear, Cindy Pace, Monica Parham, Jimmie Paschall, Cara Peck, Donna Pedro,

Hy Pomerance, LaTonia Pouncey, Danyale Price, Susan Reid, Eiry Roberts, Dwight Robinson, Christine Rogers-Raetsch, Aida Sabo, Deborah Rosado Shaw, Meisha Sherman, Ellyn Shook, Maria Stolfi, Rana Strellis, Karen Sumberg, Brian Tippens, NV "Tiger" Tyagarajan, Vera Vitels, Lynn O'Connor Vos, Barbara Wankoff, Jennifer Welty, and Nadia Younes.

Thanks also to Melissa Arnoldi, Ella Bell, Keisha Bell, Stephanie Bird, Susan Chapman-Hughes, Joanna Coles, Angela Daker, Denise Diallo, Janna Ducich, Tiffany Eubanks-Saunders, Queenie Gandy, Belinda Grant-Anderson, Valerie Grillo, Mellody Hobson, Melissa James, Charlene Drew Jarvis, Risa Lavizzo-Mourey, Sandy Lucas, Julie Marcello, Karla Martin, Glenda McNeal, Yvette Miley, Marvy Moore, Stephanie Parker, Monica Poindexter, Julie Pope, Desiree Ralls-Morrison, Trisch Smith, Denise Strauss, Geri Thomas, Joyce Trimuel, Isabel Gomez Vidal, Wanji Walcott, Pia Wilson-Body, and the women and men who took part in focus groups and Insights In-Depth® sessions.

ADDITIONAL PUBLICATIONS

KEEPING TALENTED WOMEN ON THE ROAD TO SUCCESS

The Power of the Purse: Engaging Women Decision Makers for Healthy Outcomes
Sponsors: Aetna, Bristol-Myers Squibb, Cardinal Health, Eli Lilly and Company, Johnson & Johnson, Merck & Co., Merck KGaA, MetLife, Pfizer, PwC, Strategy&, Teva, WPP (2015)

Women Want Five Things
Sponsors: American Express, AT&T, Bank of America, Boehringer Ingelheim USA, Merck KGaA, The Moody's Foundation (2014)

Harnessing the Power of the Purse: Female Investors and Global Opportunities for Growth
Sponsors: Credit Suisse, Deutsche Bank, Goldman Sachs, Morgan Stanley, Standard Chartered Bank, UBS (2014)

Executive Presence: The Missing Link between Merit and Success
HarperCollins, June 2014

Forget a Mentor, Find a Sponsor: The New Way to Fast-Track Your Career
Harvard Business Review Press, September 2013

On-Ramps and Up-Ramps India
Sponsors: Citi, Genpact, Sodexo, Standard Chartered Bank, Unilever (2013)

Executive Presence
Sponsors: American Express, Bloomberg LP, Credit Suisse, Ernst & Young, Gap Inc., Goldman Sachs, Interpublic Group, The Moody's Foundation (2012)

Sponsor Effect 2.0: Road Maps for Sponsors and Protégés
Sponsors: American Express, AT&T, Booz Allen Hamilton, Deloitte, Freddie Mac, Genentech, Morgan Stanley (2012)

Sponsor Effect: UK
Sponsor: Lloyds Banking Group (2012)

Off-Ramps and On-Ramps Japan: Keeping Talented Women on the Road to Success
Sponsors: Bank of America, Cisco, Goldman Sachs (2011)

The Relationship You Need to Get Right
Harvard Business Review, October 2011

Sponsor Effect: Breaking Through the Last Glass Ceiling
Sponsors: American Express, Deloitte, Intel, Morgan Stanley (2010)

Off-Ramps and On-Ramps Revisited
Harvard Business Review, June 2010

Off-Ramps and On-Ramps Revisited
Sponsors: Cisco, Ernst & Young, The Moody's Foundation (2010)

Letzte Ausfahrt Babypause
Harvard Business Manager (Germany), May 2010

Off-Ramps and On-Ramps Germany
Sponsors: Boehringer Ingelheim, Deutsche Bank, Siemens AG (2010)

Off-Ramps and On-Ramps: Keeping Talented Women on the Road to Success
Harvard Business Review Press, 2007

Off-Ramps and On-Ramps: Keeping Talented Women on the Road to Success
Harvard Business Review, March 2005

The Hidden Brain Drain: Off-Ramps and On-Ramps in Women's Careers
Sponsors: Ernst & Young, Goldman Sachs, Lehman Brothers (2005)

LEVERAGING MINORITY AND MULTICULTURAL TALENT

Black Women: Ready to Lead
Sponsors: American Express, AT&T, Bank of America, Chubb
Group of Insurance Companies, The Depository Trust &
Clearing Corporation, Intel, Morgan Stanley, White & Case
LLP (2015)

**How Diversity Drives Innovation: A Compendium of Best
Practices**
Sponsors: Bloomberg LP, Bristol-Myers Squibb, Cisco,
Deutsche Bank, EY, Siemens AG, Time Warner (2014)

**Cracking the Code: Executive Presence and Multicultural
Professionals**
Sponsors: Bank of America, Chubb Group of Insurance
Companies, Deloitte, GE, Intel Corporation, McKesson
Corporation (2013)

How Diversity Can Drive Innovation
Harvard Business Review, December 2013

Innovation, Diversity and Market Growth
Sponsors: Bloomberg LP, Bristol-Myers Squibb, Cisco,
Deutsche Bank, EY, Siemens AG, Time Warner (2013)

**Vaulting the Color Bar: How Sponsorship Levers
Multicultural Professionals into Leadership**
Sponsors: American Express, Bank of America, Bristol-Myers
Squibb, Deloitte, Intel, Morgan Stanley, NBCUniversal (2012)

**Asians in America: Unleashing the Potential of the "Model
Minority"**
Sponsors: Deloitte, Goldman Sachs, Pfizer, Time Warner (2011)

Sin Fronteras: Celebrating and Capitalizing on the Strengths of Latina Executives
Sponsors: Booz Allen Hamilton, Cisco, Credit Suisse, General Electric, Goldman Sachs, Johnson & Johnson, Time Warner (2007)

Global Multicultural Executives and the Talent Pipeline
Sponsors: Citigroup, General Electric, PepsiCo, Time Warner, Unilever (2008)

Leadership in Your Midst: Tapping the Hidden Strengths of Minority Executives
Harvard Business Review, November 2005

Invisible Lives: Celebrating and Leveraging Diversity in the Executive Suite
Sponsors: General Electric, Time Warner, Unilever (2005)

Forthcoming 2016: Latinos in the US

Realizing the Full Potential of LGBT Talent

Out in the World: Securing LGBT Rights in the Global Marketplace
Sponsors: American Express, Bank of America, Barclays, Bloomberg LP, BNY Mellon, BP, Chubb, Deutsche Bank, Eli Lilly and Company, Ernst & Young LLP, and Out Leadership (2016)

The Power of "Out" 2.0: LGBT in the Workplace
Sponsors: Deloitte, Out on the Street, Time Warner (2013)

For LGBT Workers, Being "Out" Brings Advantages
Harvard Business Review, July/August 2011

The Power of "Out": LGBT in the Workplace
Sponsors: American Express, Boehringer Ingelheim USA, Cisco, Credit Suisse, Deloitte, Google (2011)

Retaining and Sustaining Top Talent

Mission Critical: Unlocking the Value of Vets in the Workforce
Sponsors: Booz Allen Hamilton, Boehringer Ingelheim USA,
Fordham University, Intercontinental Exchange/NYSE,
Prudential Financial, The Moody's Foundation, Wounded
Warrior Project (2015)

Top Talent: Keeping Performance Up When Business Is Down
Harvard Business Press, 2009

Sustaining High Performance in Difficult Times
Sponsor: The Moody's Foundation (2008)

Seduction and Risk: The Emergence of Extreme Jobs
Sponsors: American Express, BP plc, ProLogis, UBS (2007)

Extreme Jobs: The Dangerous Allure of the 70-Hour Workweek
Harvard Business Review, December 2006

Forthcoming 2017: Disrupting Bias, Uncovering Value

Tapping Into the Strengths of Gen Y, Gen X, and Boomers

The X Factor: Tapping into the Strengths of the 33- to 46-Year-Old Generation
Sponsors: American Express, Boehringer Ingelheim USA,
Cisco, Credit Suisse, Google (2011)

How Gen Y & Boomers Will Reshape Your Agenda
Harvard Business Review, July/August 2009

Bookend Generations: Leveraging Talent and Finding Common Ground
Sponsors: Booz Allen Hamilton, Ernst & Young, Lehman
Brothers, Time Warner, UBS (2009)

Forthcoming 2016: Misunderstood Millennials

BECOMING A TALENT MAGNET IN EMERGING MARKETS

Growing Global Executives: The New Competencies
Sponsors: American Express, Bloomberg LP, Cisco Systems, EY, Genpact, Goldman Sachs, Intel, Pearson, Sodexo, The Moody's Foundation (2015)

The Battle for Female Talent in Brazil
Sponsors: Bloomberg LP, Booz & Company, Intel, Pfizer, Siemens AG (2011)

Winning the War for Talent in Emerging Markets
Harvard Business Press, August 2011

The Battle for Female Talent in China
Sponsors: Bloomberg LP, Booz & Company, Intel, Pfizer, Siemens AG (2010)

The Battle for Female Talent in India
Sponsors: Bloomberg LP, Booz & Company, Intel, Pfizer, Siemens AG (2010)

The Battle for Female Talent in Emerging Markets
Harvard Business Review, May 2010

PREVENTING THE EXODUS OF WOMEN IN SET

Athena Factor 2.0: Accelerating Female Talent in Science, Engineering & Technology
Sponsors: American Express, Boehringer Ingelheim USA, BP, Genentech, McKesson Corporation, Merck Serono, Schlumberger, Siemens AG (2014)

The Under-Leveraged Talent Pool: Women Technologists on Wall Street
Sponsors: Bank of America, Credit Suisse, Goldman Sachs, Intel, Merrill Lynch, NYSE Euronext (2008)

Stopping the Exodus of Women in Science
Harvard Business Review, June 2008

The Athena Factor: Reversing the Brain Drain in Science, Engineering, and Technology
Sponsors: Alcoa, Cisco, Johnson & Johnson, Microsoft, Pfizer (2008)

TASK FORCE FOR TALENT INNOVATION

INDEX

ABOUT THE AUTHORS

Melinda Marshall is executive vice president and director of publications at the Center for Talent Innovation, where she drives the Center's research on innovation, sponsorship, and leadership. She has coauthored articles for the *Harvard Business Review*, including "How Diversity Can Drive Innovation" and "The Relationship You Need to Get Right" and CTI reports including *Innovation, Diversity and Market Growth* as well as *Sponsor Effect 2.0*. Her most recent blog, "Looking for Innovation in All the Wrong Places," appeared in the *Stanford Social Innovation Review*. Having completed *Women Want Five Things*, a study of women's ambition and relationship to power, she helped drive the Center's eleven-country study of leadership competencies (*Growing Global Executives: The New Competencies*) and *Out in the World: Securing LGBT Rights in the Global Marketplace*. A journalist, editor, and former national humor columnist, she has published eleven books in collaboration, and is the author of the award-winning *Good Enough Mothers: Changing Expectations for Ourselves*. Her articles have appeared in eighteen national magazines, including the *Harvard Business Review*, *Parenting*, and *Ladies Home Journal*. A magna cum laude graduate of Duke University, she earned her Master's in Human Rights Studies at Columbia University.

Tai Wingfield is senior vice president of communications for the Center for Talent Innovation and managing director at Hewlett Consulting Partners, where she drives corporate reputation efforts on behalf of each brand. She is an expert communicator and has effectively counseled public and private organizations on various issues including brand reputation management and awareness, minority outreach, and human rights. She is coauthor of the CTI report *Black Women: Ready to Lead*. Previously, she worked as a member of Edelman's Business + Social Purpose practice and served as the day-to-day client contact and lead on various accounts, driving strategy development and implementation for organizations including AMD, eBay, Xylem, and Microsoft Retail. Wingfield graduated from the University of Maryland with a BA in communication and an emphasis in public relations.